Two Old Bats and a Delinquent Dog

Fiona Hewitt

Two Old Bats and a Delinquent Dog

Fiona Hewitt

HAYLOFT PUBLISHING LTD

First published 2004
Re-printed 2006

Hayloft Publishing Ltd, Kirkby Stephen,
Cumbria, CA17 4DJ

tel: (017683) 42300
fax. (017683) 41568
e-mail: books@hayloft.org.uk
web: www.hayloft.org.uk

ISBN 1 904524 17 6

A catalogue record for this book is available
from the British Library

Produced in Great Britain
Printed and bound in Hungary

Jacket illustration by Paul Gurney
Cartoons by Allan Elliott

Dedication

Thanks to my dad who hauled me up mountains as a child and Derek who taught me to love the Lakes. And   obviously to Kath - best friend and walking buddy.

Contents

The Bob Graham Round

Introduction

So how did all this come about? Well I was married to Derek who, along with many of his friends, thinks it's fun to run up and down big mountains in poor weather wearing scraps of nylon, ie he is both a nutter and a fell runner. Kath and I are both sane fell walkers and Jacko was fourteen but used to like anything that got him out of the house and within begging distance of a sandwich. We are also big fans of the Wainwright guide books.

One winter's night a few of us were slumped in from of The Bill and Derek and Woodsy were discussing 'The Bob Graham Round'. Bob Graham was a mountain guide from just south of Keswick who, in 1932, inaugurated the round shown opposite. It includes 42 peaks spread over 72 miles and should be run in under 24 hours. Rumour has it Graham himself ran this barefoot as part of his training.

"You and Kath should do that," Derek said, "walk it as a route." So we did. We started on 15 August 1994 and finished on 8 February 1997 - only two and a half years slower than Bob! This is our story.

Lost Dogs, Suicidal Ramblings and the Emergency Cross

Five minutes before eleven o'clock and we're stood outside the clock tower in Keswick, on a hot August day in 1984. Kathryn and I are eagerly awaiting the striking of eleven so that we can start on our epic. We had planned an earlier start but just to be on the safe side, we had sought extra sustenance at one of the excellent tea shops in the town. As we filled our faces with cream cakes and mugs of tea we both felt entirely justified. Harking back to my Home Economics degree (let's face it, I don't often find a use for it.) I, with authority announced, "Sugar for short release energy, fat for later when the going gets tough and lots of liquid to prevent de-hydration." Kathryn nodded thoughtfully, sucking the crumbs off a finger she had just run over her plate

Yes, and it's also a sort of celebration of the launch of this epic achievement. Satisfied that we had approached this in a far more considered way than any fell runner, who, in my experience prepare for big race events with gallons of water, swigged from plastic pop bottles that has been allowed to warm up for hours in the back seat of the car and plates of pasta, we ordered more tea, a plate of tea cakes between us (we're not greedy after all) and sat back to chat a little longer.

So here we were at eleven instead of ten, filled with anticipation (and tea), waiting for the off. Jacko was hurling himself about on the end of his lead in a manner that was erratic even by his standards. At first we imagined that he could sense our tension down the lead but in fact he was just risking death by strangulation to get at a discarded chip wrapper that lay tantalisingly just beyond his reach.

The clock struck and off we went, full of vim and vigour. Two minutes later Kathryn's laces were undone, five minutes later I had to stop and remove my sweater. Yes, I know it was August and very, very hot but I've been warned about how cold these mountains were. I now had a bulging rucksack and a mouth full of puce and lime mohair (thanks mum) but I was cool and we were off again being dragged through Keswick by a manic Jack

Russell anxious to be any where but back in the car.

Getting out of Keswick was tricky but when we stopped gossiping and applied ourselves to Wainwright's little guide book and the map, we found Spooney Green Lane. From there we headed for the lower slopes of Latrigg. I have to admit that, even at this point, I was filled with mild concern. You see Latrigg does not have happy memories for me. Traditionally Latrigg fell race falls on the day after the Borrowdale race. Two races in one day is madness in itself but the Borrowdale is not just a twelve mile hike through bogs and over peaks that fell runners do most days of the year. No, this is a monster. Sixteen miles up and down huge peaks which tests even the best and causes serious health risk to the, 'I've done a bit of training, I'll be fine' type.

The highlight of this event involves drinking vast amounts of alcohol in a sweaty marquee dancing wildly to a steel band. Those who make Latrigg therefore are either very serious competitors or very short tempered due to a hang over from hell. It is therefore not the race to learn how to mark up the results board. I didn't realise this when I agreed to help Chris, a fell running friend who has many excellent qualities, organisation not being one of them. I was left with a hazy idea of what was going on and an electronic gadget. This is always fatal! I still twitch nervously when my mobile rings in

As we filled our faces with cream cakes and mugs of tea, we both felt entirely justified.

public. This thing got stuck somehow and kept printing the times and numbers on top of each other making it impossible to read. The racers began to come in, tired and sweaty, and Chris was nowhere to be seen. I did my best but was quickly swamped by over-competitive parents shouting, "Johnny was inside forty minutes, I should know I timed him and this watch came from Birmingham." (Birmingham?). Worse still were friends who were trying to be patient while I pulled the results out of a hat and grinned in what I hoped was an endearing manner. The shame of this has scarred me for life and I had not returned to Latrigg until now.

This time however the journey passed uneventfully and we enjoyed the pleasant path around Latrigg. Ok, we felt a bit bloated and slightly sick but, hell it was a worthy sacrifice, we knew that we would need the energy later. We chatted about people we knew and generally felt at one with the world, that is until we reached the road by the water works car park. Jacko had been off the lead for some time. He has never chased sheep and generally careers around us in gay abandon. There are though three passions in Jacko's life: Food of any quality or variety except oddly enough lettuce and alcohol, and the desire to get outside and roll in the excrement of other animals are the two hobbies most often witnessed. There is however one other, which once it has taken him, means that he can not be distracted even by the other two. His little doggy brain empties, not a long job I grant you, and is filled with one obsessive, compulsive impulse: RABBITS!

Also when Jacko decides to misbehave, boy does he love an audience. It being a hot day, as I have already said and Skiddaw being a popular tourist trap, a sizeable crowd had gathered in the car park. I was climbing over the style by the fence with as much dignity as possible when there was a flash of brown with a little white tail. This in itself was unbalancing enough but when it was closely pursued by two stones of fluff and enthusiasm bolting as fast as is possible on seven inch legs I completely lost my footing and landed in a painful heap only too aware of the not so muffled amusement of the crowd. There was no time for embarrassment however as I had seen this type of response before and I knew we were in trouble. I set off trundling after him, cursing under my breath, rucksack bouncing and most definitely regretting the cream cake.

Kathryn, although mystified at first, sensed the urgency and off we went, urged on by so called humourous comments from the now enthralled crowd. "Ten to one on the little fellow" sticks in my memory as a particularly wounding remark. Of course Jacko shot into the woods of the new plantation and was quickly lost from view. Ten minutes of futile calling, including alternating wheedling and cursing was to no avail. The undergrowth in that wood is quite dense and the bank is steep. You slither down hill on the pine needles, held in place only by viscous brambles. These clutch your ankles and calves causing great bleeding weals on your fake tanned legs. As if this was not enough, larch branches whip back at your face and clutch at your hair. Just as I was getting desperate and, I feel our friend ship was being tested to the limit, Kathryn and I spotted the little beggar. We watched powerlessly, furious to see Jacko bolt for cover, grinning all over his face and not ten yards below us. He turned and for a moment we thought he had remembered a shred of obedience. Fat chance. Instead he belted past us tongue lolling and ecstasy written all over his face and, horror of horrors, ran off UP HILL! No more wheedling now, not enough breath. We did still manage lots of obscenities as we slogged painfully back up the route we had just come, encountering all the savage vegetation which once again whipped us without mercy. Jacko of course being only thirteen inches from the floor scampered underneath it all completely unscathed, git! Needless to say that as we emerged at the top by the fence, bruised, scratched, furious and exhausted Jacko popped into view again way below us by the stream. All would have ended in violence had Kathryn not had a brain wave.

Noticing that Jacko himself now seemed a little less determined and guessing that he had probably forgotten why he was running she decided to apply to his other passions. She picked up a discarded crisp packet from the floor (I will never curse litter louts again) and began to rustle it vigorously. At first it seemed that nothing had happened, then Jacko pricked up the one ear that he can prick up and he listened. Not daring to move I stood transfixed and Kathryn rustled the packet with all the verve of a novice tambourine player at a Salvation Army rally. After what seemed like an aeon, he turned his fat little body

towards us and, eyes on the crisp packet began to gallop sham-
bolically towards us. When we finally got hold of him, he was
severely chastised but he didn't care. He wriggled free and
stuck his nose into the packet greedily licking up any remaining
traces of salt.

Jacko now safely back on the lead, we set off up the great
scar that is the path up this mountain. I have massive double
standards about the ecological damage caused by walkers. On
the one hand I am horrified by the gashes like this one carved
into what is the oldest mountain in the area. It offers splendid
views, which differ greatly depending on which way you face on
the summit, and contributes a lot to the geological interest in
Cumbria. In short it demands more respect. On the other hand
I am part of the problem and I'm not willing to stop. The marvellous work of the National Trust path builders does help but
they are not the whole answer and I don't know what is. Enough
preaching and back to the plot.

Wainwright describes Skiddaw as an easy climb; it would seem
to be so for the multitude passing me on the way up. For me
however, woefully unfit, already exhausted, thirsty and out of
sorts from our earlier exploits, I found every step an effort.
While the assorted hoards aged from two to ninety two surged
upwards laughing and chatting, I seemed to slip backward on the
loose scree more than I moved forwards. Sweat dripped off me
into my socks making my feet sore and I had to stop every ten
yards. Kathryn by comparison leapt up the slopes like a bloody
gazelle on steroids, chatting pleasantly to all comers.
Throughout this epic both of us hit low points when it all just
seemed like a trudge. Walking, much like running I'm reliably
informed, depends as much on the mind as it does on the legs
and the lungs and if all three pack in at once, as Bart Simpson
says, "You're in deep deep trouble." The only way through is to
distract yourself and my favourite way of doing this is to list
boys and girls names beginning with different letters of the
alphabet. OK so I've never yet met a guy called Yoland or a girl
called Xyla but to admit mental as well as physical melt down
would have pushed the self esteem meter into the red bit
marked, 'lie down and die' and I had a hill to climb.

Onwards, ever onwards, I climbed pausing only to pay homage
to the small ruin that was once a refreshment hut. (How cruel

time can be). Eventually the ground began to level out a bit and remembering my husband's advice to go round the Little Man rather than over it we headed off to the right. Sadly an error of judgement and criminal disregard for the map meant that instead of skirting Skiddaw Little Man we were skirting Jenkins Hill. When we changed our minds and went up it, tempted by the idea of checking Skiddaw Little Man off our list of peaks, we found ourselves looking at it in the distance. We did try to cheat the map to make Skiddaw Little Man into its big brother but to no avail and off we went again. Once we had supposedly reached Skiddaw Little Man, it was obvious that this wasn't the real thing either as that loomed off into distance.

Off we toddled again, the end, or so we thought in sight. We got to the top of the next little rise only to be disappointed yet again; it was only the south top. I ask you how much more can two knackered women and a deranged dog take? This time there was no way I could fool myself for, on the next little rise, the hoards were gathered clambering over the trig point and taking pictures. Jacko at least was delighted, he had caught the scent of meat paste sandwiches on the wind and that was better than any map. It was, once again, a case of follow that white streak. Finally we achieved our first peak, Skiddaw. It is a very impressive mountain with wonderful views but what with the dog's antics and my appaling route planning (and I use the word planning in its loosest sense) we were well behind time. We just had time for the dog to beg unashamedly and for each of us to devour our rationed snacks. Kathryn tucked into her pastrami and watercress on wholemeal bread while I munched blissfully on a squashed, warm, egg mayonnaise butty, food of the Gods!

Peak number two was clearly in view. Great Calva is delightfully distinctive in shape but even so, we were taking no chances. Only after two compass bearings, reading the guide book and thoroughly studying the map did we set off towards Hare Crag and up the purple slopes of hill number two, Great Calva. This is a pleasant summit and was by far the best of the day. We quickly ticked off the summit and headed for the wonderfully convenient shelter for much needed sustenance. The shelter however was not empty but we are both sociable people so we huddled in beside the lone stranger. Our new companion was not pleased to see us to say the least. He was a young lad of pale hue, painfully thin in that fashionable way that suggests a serious wasting disease. His limp blonde hair hung in two trendy little curtains over his downcast face in the way that is meant to indicate a deep sensitive personality but that more often denotes a self indulgent, vapid weariness caused by the usual teenage angst or too much self abuse.

"I came here to be alone," he whined petulantly.

"Oh I know," Kathryn exclaimed, full of life, "We both love the less popular hills."

"No," he continued, "I've got a few problems and I came here to think."

"Good place for thinking, the hills," I responded, "Would you like a banana?" He looked at me in horror as I peeled the fruit and handed it absent mindedly to him. Like a rabbit trapped in the headlights he reached for the fruit. At that moment Jacko reappeared, having been rolling in something particularly malodorous, probably a rotting sheep or a dead seagull's entrails. Either way he shot into the shelter at full pelt, back legs round his ears. He skidded round the corner, eyed the youth beadily, leapt into the air grasping the banana in his vice like, little jaw and, turning with surprising agility for one so stout, pelted out of the shelter to enjoy his ill-gotten gains.

"He sometimes does that," said Kathryn with tremendous sang froid.

The poor youth, there he was wallowing in wonderful adolescent misery, flirting dramatically with near suicidal thoughts and what happens? Two gossiping, rudely cheerful, middle-aged women interrupt him, force-feed him with fruit and then he is robbed by a quite probably aggressive, war like beast coated in crap. Just when he felt that life could get no worse!

Through our whole traipse around the route, the next thirty minutes were the longest. In fact and I began to identify with the feelings of the youth we had just left. I would go so far as to say that they were the longest thirty minutes of my whole life including those at the end of the second half of 'Les Mis' as performed by the Local Rep. Mungrizedale is just a plod across boggy, uneven terrain. It's a bit like being on one of those moving pathways you find at airports, but instead of going much faster than you can walk, allowing you to carry on walking and really pick up speed, it goes so slow that you end up further and further away from your destination. Wainwright describes it as having natural attractions of a type that, 'appeals only to sheep' and we saw two of them trying to slit their wrists. Oh well here we go: Andrew, Brian Charles, Edward, Fredric, George... Suffice to say that after at least one polar ice cap had melted and I had made serious inroads into the menopause, we did get across it.

Next on the list is Blencathra, a sneaky favourite of mine but Kathryn's worst nightmare given that on our last two ascents of this mountain we had had bad experiences. On the first Kathryn felt bad before we started but we decided to persevere out of the misplaced belief that 'things would be OK' once we got going. Half way up Kathryn, who is of all the people I know the one least given to hysteria, told me that she felt faint. We were at the time clinging to a rock on Hall's Fell with our teeth and toe-nails having unintentionally chosen 'a more exciting deviation.' She was temporarily appeased with two custard creams and a Garibaldi but when we descended via Doddick Gill (well it looked straight forward at the top but is described as, 'Hard scrambling throughout, For tough guys only, Not to be used for descent') that Kathryn's very genuine case of vertigo raised its head again.

Our second attempt had mainly involved us floundering down Sharp Edge in thick mist. So, all in all Kathryn was not looking forward to Blencathra.

In the event however the ascent went well, yes we were tired but, hey, this was our last fell today, the car was in the next valley and we had left a packet of jaffa cakes in the boot. We clambered up a nice little path near Atkinson Fell and there we were on the top of our last fell!

Blencathra is a splendid mountain, it is in no way a hill or peak, it's a mountain. It is immediately recognisable from lots of different angles and from quite a distance away. It can be dangerous and for this and for its sheer bulk it commands respect. Given that we were shattered and had parked our car by the Blencathra Centre, we decided to walk along the summit and walk off down the shoulder known as Blease Fell. We thought it would be easier than any of the ridges! We strolled along the fabulous top, discussing the Bob Graham Round. "Do you really mean to tell me that people run this bloody route?" Kathryn asked

"Yes, well most of it," I replied. "Mind you they do have someone else to carry all their food."

"What, all of it?"

"Yes."

We looked at each other knowingly, we would need to book a team of bloody Sherpas for just today's meagre rations and we had only done three of the forty-five peaks.

"Of course they can do it which ever way round they want. They can either go through what we've just done at the beginning and get it over and done with," I said.

"And realise immediately what a bloody ridiculous idea it is, pack up and go home in time for Changing Places," Kathryn muttered.

"Or," I continued undaunted, "they can run another 39 peaks then run these three just to finish it all off nicely."

Kathryn looked at me for a minute then asked, "And you knew all this before you agreed to marry Derek?"

The black gloom I had been fighting off descended a little further over my shoulders. Looking around for something to improve our spirits I glanced left and immediately lost the will to live. Kathryn, with her usual perception, noticed when I gasped and fell to my knees.

"Don't worry," she soothed, "you could always leave him."

"No, it's not that," I croaked through taut lips which had gone white and from which a tiny fleck of rabid foam had dribbled, "Look I pointed to the mass of rock that towered upwards on the other side of the road, unable to control my quivering digit."

"What? It is just another... Oh my God, you don't mean to tell me... Get the map!" I didn't like the way her voice was escalating, she usually so calm and dependable. "That's our next peak isn't it? That's Clough Head."

"I... I think so. And when we've done that one there are eight more to go before we finish that leg."

"Do you really, really mean to tell me that people run this bloody route?"

"Yes, I told you they do all 72 miles, 27 thousand feet of accent and 42 peaks in under 24 hours."

"Flaming madness!" she muttered and shrugged her rucksack

further up her back in a self righteous way I had seen before and knew better than to argue with. I decided that silence was the best plan and fell into step behind her. I swear that top went on for miles. We seemed to walk for hours and if we looked forwards we could see how very much further we had to go, if we looked right we could see bloody Skiddaw. If we looked backwards we could see flaming Mungrizedale Common and if we looked left, well that didn't bear thinking about. I did consider closing my eyes but I worried that I may wander of track and never see civilisation again. After a while even that concern ceased to matter and my mind drifted off to a world where Wham were still together and you could buy a gin and tonic for a pound. My knees, always poor on descents, felt that they would snap. Suddenly, quite abruptly we both sat down, it was like telepathy between two drowning souls, and we just flopped on the floor.

"I can't go any further," I whined.

"I know Fee, I know. Perhaps we could stay here."

"Right here? For ever?" I pleaded hopefully.

"Yes," She said with a resigned air of finality.

It seemed like a good plan to me and we lay back in the sun to wait for... something.

We had been lying there for some time when we heard a whirring noise up above.

"Quick!" she shouted with more enthusiasm than I had ever hoped to see again. "Make a cross!"

Now both of us are under five foot four and we are not light. Generous, curvaceous, even ample I would accept. If we lay across each other we would be too short to make a cross but would instead resemble a nasty road accident. Also there was the added risk that whoever had to go underneath would have to spend the rest of their days on an iron lung. If we didn't lie across one another we could only make half a cross and the message we would send to the helicopter pilot would not encourage him to swoop to our assistance. We did try to faff about with our rucksacks but by then we were laughing so much that the chopper was almost over us. Just as well probably because when we had a good look at it, it was trailing a long banner advertising, 'Fun flights from Blackpool.'

This did cheer us up and we staggered painfully back to the

car only to find a message from the police.

"Typical," Kathryn said in tones of hurt pride, "They have looked me up on the computer and found out that I am a sofa squatter, found outside only in restaurants and tea rooms. Naturally they wouldn't expect to find me here, they think the damn thing's been nicked!"

All Days Should Be Like This

Kathryn and I were a little daunted by this trip for a number of reasons. Firstly, the memories of the previous epic were still etched in our minds, in particular the image of Clough Head rearing up from the valley. Secondly, there are some pretty big hills in this section, several in fact are over 2,500 feet and one over 3000 feet. We could have coped with this by opting for our usual tactic of burying our heads in the sand and thinking of something else but for one thing - Debby.

Debby was a colleague from work who had expressed an interest in joining us on one of our trips for some time. No problem. In fact, the more the merrier, usually. Debby, however had recently been on one of these, 'wonder diets.' You know the type of thing, you drink one glass of chemicals a day and, for a treat you get a cardboard fibre bar once a week. At first your bowels are so active that the mere sight of a Labrador puppy makes you flea to the loo then your whole anal tract self seals and atrophies while your stomach shrinks to the size of a walnut. After that, it seems you merely assimilate nutrients from the atmosphere and never crave fried egg sandwiches again. Something like that anyway. To be honest anything that spoils the pure joy that is eating has never appealed

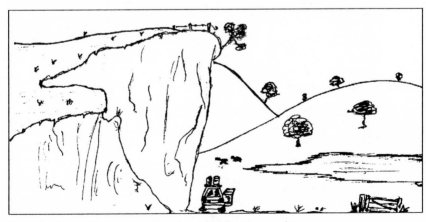

Disused quarries are not only ugly they're sad.too.

at all. Anyway, Debby, who had previously had a similar protective layer of flesh to us, now resembled a Russian gymnast - all muscles and sinews. Debby's husband had always been one of those super fit climbing, running, outdoors in all weather types and recently Debby had joined him. "Do you know that I can now run the drive in under six minutes?" she purred.

'I can't even drive it in that' I thought, thinking how my darling little £150 Fiesta would cope if I even whispered such a notion within fifty feet of its rusty little bonnet.

"Why run down the drive at all?" Kathryn asked. "The very name of such a track dictates its proper use."

Anyhow, we had left Debby's gleaming Audi at the top of Dunmail Raise and were heading north in the Fiesta. The loud whine, which for weeks I had been dismissing as, 'a leaf trapped against the fan' but was I knew deep down the final death throws of a car that has given up hope. The slight smell of burning oil did not distract Kathryn or me from the obvious fact. We were going to climb about ten huge mountains, accompanied by an athlete. This was not helped by the fact that, in order to cope with this daunting situation we had all gone out on a 'staff do' the night before and had single handedly raised the share index for Gordon's gin to it's highest ever point. The afore-mentioned fumes, total lack of suspension and queasy fear were doing nothing for my head or stomach.

We pulled up in the little quarry car park and made a show of warming up. Having clutched at my ankle behind my bottom a few times, wobbling perilously on one leg, in order to stretch my hamstrings (I have only ever had a vague notion of where and what hamstrings are but in the face of desperation it seemed like a good idea at the time. Also it delayed the start for a while. I was now exhausted. Debby on the other hand threw herself into a full-scale aerobic work out. I collapsed against the car causing the suspension to wheeze and Kathryn looked quizzical for a while, shrugged philosophically, then got out her sandwiches and joined me on the bank.

A while later we began to meander round the quarry. I know that the Lake District is or was a working community. I know that it provided many much-needed jobs. God damn it I even love the lovely green slate produced at Honister and displayed at its best as the surface of the bar in the Borrowdale pub but

I still find quarries ugly beyond belief. Disused ones are not only ugly, they're sad too. All that rusting, obsolete machinery sitting in muddy, dead puddles and the tyre tracks of old vehicles hardened into gouged ruts. It's horrible. Sometimes you get uplifted by a tiny yew tree clinging from the cliff face but more often then not the patch of dandelions struggling futilely to grow among the rubble only makes the whole scene more melancholy. The whole thing did little to raise our spirits.

However once on the old coach road track things began to pick up. The sun came out, the fresh air and exercise were driving the alcohol out of my pores and it was pleasant under foot. I like contouring, I really do. You get a long way for minimum effort, I mean that would even do as a creed for life. Also, so long as you didn't actually look right, the high mountain might not really exist. We rounded the base wiling away time in pleasant girlie chat - how does Grant Mitchell attract all those women when he looks like the missing link and has the personal charm of an old veruca plaster? Did any of our male colleagues have buttocks that could distract us from the assembly hymns and wasn't Jacko much cuter when he was chasing butterflies than when he was stalking other dogs or small children?

Eventually the time came to turn resolutely right and aim for the top. Feeling better all the time Kathryn and I dug in. We had noticed that Debby was finding it as hard as us ergo we must also be athletes! Invigorated by this crazy logic we were off. Usually I hate false summits but today they were marvellous as every time we're reached one we could sit down, drink pop, and console Debby who was worsening by the second and was by now I think in the last throws of alcoholic poisoning. Determined that she should enjoy this trip and not wanting to give up, Kathryn and I took it in turn to scamper (I kid you not) a few yards ahead then come back and cheerily announce, "Not far now." It was no good however. Debby slumped to the floor and with, an ashen face, declared that if she had had any more liquid left in her body she would have been violently sick there and then. We all sat down and came to the conclusion that Debby would return to my car, drive it to Dunmail then get back into her own and return home.

As she began to trail back down the hill, having insisted that we did not accompany her but agreeing to take most of our water with her, we turned to continue. The summit was in fact just over the next rise and we did try to call to Debby to tell her this but she just gave us a wan smile and a fragile little wave and turned to go.

It was at this point that we both turned and looked in the direction we were to go in next. We couldn't believe it, there, stretched out in front of us, wide and clear in the sun, was the path across the top of our next five peaks and it was more or less FLAT! We got the map out to check and, better and better, not only was this more or less the truth but the next two peaks after that were also more or less level with Helvellyn. The sun was warm but not oppressive, there was a delightful breeze coming from behind us, an obvious, flat path to follow and the ground was springy and soft underfoot. If we had been the type to launch into 'Val de Ree, Val de Ra' now would have been that moment. Fortunately Kathryn has too much reserve and I didn't know the words. Never the less our spirits lifted as we got 'that' feeling. Jacko, noticing that the path was littered with other walkers put on his cute face and sped off to beg for sandwiches, well aware that he would be more successful if he wasn't with us and could pretend to be a stray.

The grass flew beneath our feet and with very little effort we had climbed up the gentle ascent to Great Dodd and, an event previously not experienced by ourselves, we did not stop at all at the summit. The views are spectacular and the autumnal colours were inspiring. It really was as if our feet had wings. "Do you know, maybe we could run this bit," Kathryn whispered.

"Yes," I agreed, "this bit, yes." And off we sped into a rather shambolic trot, rucksacks bouncing around as we galumphed on for about another twenty paces before coming to a breathless giggling halt. Never let it be said that we haven't 'run the Bob Graham'. Well this bit any way.

When you walk regularly with someone, or as I've since found out through talking to other people, when you do any outdoor activity together, the bond between you changes. Whether it is because you have to rely totally on each other at times of crisis or because when one is low the other generally rallies round and gives support, I don't know. Maybe it is just that you spend so much time together that you talk about everything and I mean every thing. Whatever it is, outdoor pursuits partners are a special sort of friend and I know that many other people find this to be the case. Anyhow I can honestly say that at that moment in time I would not have been anywhere else in the world, doing anything else, in the world with anyone else in the world (except possibly my husband) for all the cash in the world. All days should be like this. We were both equally uplifted and it was brilliant. Enough mush and on with the epic.

In this frame of mind we quickly reached Watson's Dodd where we encountered Peter from Chapel en Le Frith. As a rule Kathryn and I do not talk much to other walkers. Don't get me wrong, we're not rude. We do say, "good morning" or "hello" and have been known to make cheerily inane remarks about the weather. Also when on the summit, as in the last chapter we will chat to anyone. En route, however we don't usually effuse - to be honest we can't usually spare the breath. Today however was different. Peter had a copy of a walking magazine I also sub-scribed to and that was it. We were all off on a conversation-al spree, which actually lasted until Stybarrow Dodd.

There we parted company but not before Peter had told us we should write a book about our experiences and if we did to please include him. Certainly Peter, no problem.

Kathryn at this point observed that we had now ticked off four of the peaks, seven if you added last week's and that by the end of the trip we would have done six more making a total of thirteen. My God, you can't fault that girl's maths I tell you. The views back over towards Keswick were by now beyond description. You could see for miles and miles and the colours were every shade of bronze, green and gold under a perfect blue sky. We stopped to identify distant peaks from the map and got a distinct tingle when we found that we could see most of the next leg and even some of the other peaks of this walk. This also gave Peter time to move on. Even though we were experiencing elation, there is a natural limit to any conversation with a strange man you do not want to know any better.

Next up was Raise praised by the Wainwright as, 'a welcome change from the dull monotony of the green expanses.' I am sorry but I have to disagree. As one who loves to sit down while she eats, thus combining two pleasures in one, I do not like sharp stones. I have even been known to lie in the grass on my belly, chin resting on palms and gazing out into space. Had I attempted this on Raise I would have received severe lacerations to parts of my anatomy I usually go to great lengths to conceal even from doctors. I did find somewhere to squat but I'm not really built for perching prettily on a rock. I am not a bloody garden gnome. True, by now the light on Coniston and the estuary was like a shimmering patch of magic.

This did not make up for two strange sights this peak offers. One is the bizarre sight of a ski lift crawling up one side of the hill. Believe me I love skiing but surely one of the most basic pre-requisites of this sport is, well, snow, and although we do get it up here we don't get it much, we don't get it often and it doesn't last long. Also, most foreign lift systems are within staggering distance of two things, namely a road and a site of refreshment. This site would require you to haul your skis half way up a bloody mountain, ski up and down the same patch of snow until it wore out, say thirty minutes, then haul the whole lot back down the mountain with not a gluwein in sight. Mmm sounds just perfect to me. If you're of the masochistic personality type that also enjoys wallpaper stripping and eats pop tarts out of choice.

The other not too edifying site is Helvellyn. I'm sure that Helvellyn is a very beautiful mountain. Why shouldn't it be? It has two lovely ridge approaches, one leading to the fabulously precarious Catstycam. It has the beautiful Red Tarn and it has tremendous views. What it also has, absolutely always, is a lot of other people. Yes, I know that to them I'm other people and I would defend their right to be there with my dying breath but they change a wild and potentially dangerous fell top into a sort of open air rock concert without music. Also, I once had the misfortune to be there with a so called bloody mystic refugee from Glastonbury or similar haunt for whom reality is something with which they only occasionally collide. This particular specimen sat cross legged on top of the trig point playing some sort of pan pipes very badly. He/she smiled beatifically at me mistaking my relief that at least it wasn't one of the genre who felt it necessary to also shed their clothing, for appreciation of his 'music.' I tell you now Lady in Red has never seemed so scary.

Today was no exception, the dog went into a begging frenzy, fought with at least two other dogs and peed on the trig point which was at the time surrounded by what looked like a

Japanese football team. I just hope their Nikon shutters had all clicked before he gleefully raised his leg and obligingly smiled at the camera. I developed a strange craving for a Macdonald's burger and Kathryn had to be curbed from singing You'll never Walk Alone. This is one mountain where you can always see examples of all the available types of walker.

First there is the tourist who falls into one of two categories. There are the Japanese, seen all over the Lake District, usually in packs of at least eight. They always have gear that makes you green with envy, contribute a small fortune to our Cumbrian economy, are invariably polite with well behaved children and they never get so drunk in hostels that they cry on your shoulder or throw up on your car. You don't usually see them outside shopping areas but some do escape to the hills. Next up are the English bank holiday crew. Again these hunt in large family groups. The mothers sit at the top of popular crags discussing their internal plumbing, the children play football on steep ledges and the fathers join in until they get puffed then they sit gasping while their tummies turn a painful shade of puce, unaccustomed to exposure to the sun. Adolescent specimens wear jeans and carry bags of potatoes up Helvellyn in November hoping to find enough wood up there to cook these vegetables.

The other extreme is the gear freak, inevitably male. This man, usually between 28 and 48 carries everything and a spare of everything. Dressed completely in Berghaus, he won't walk round Brother's Water without a tent, a spare tent, two sleeping bags, a flare and a spare flare. He is the only person you will ever see actually eating Kendal Mint Cake. Modern versions have both a mobile phone and a GPS navigator. The opposite to this is the fell runner who wears a tiny light weight vest and indecent micro shorts and, reluctantly, carries anything else in a tiny bum bag. His, or increasingly often her, emergency provisions include a scrunched up power bar the wrapper of which doubles as a cagoule. Only in very wild country will he carry a map and even then it will be a two-inch square cut from an old OS map of Bingley town centre. Finally there is the type I most admire, the old timer. Males wear checked shirts and knee britches seemingly cut from old blankets. They have leathery tans, maps in their heads and hurtle up very steep hills whistling to very old or even imaginary sheep dogs. The females, the group I aspire to, usually wear tweed suits of a heathery shade, fleshy tights and sensible shoes. They occasionally use walking sticks, which they wave at grizzled old terriers while holding forth on the good old days in Brown Owl voices. They are also incredibly robust. This paragraph may sound as though I'm taking the Mickey, I'm not, remember I started this journey in a lime green and puce mohair jumper and Kathryn never ventures onto the hills without her own little delicatessen. We all have our foibles, I know someone who always takes his teddy bear with him and someone else who won't even go to the shops without full make up. Humans are a diverse bunch and you find most types on top of Helvellyn.

Having negotiated these people and paddled through the lolly wrappers old cans and fag ends we left this poor old prostitute of a mountain, both humming popular songs from Radio One for some strange reason. Helvellyn can do that to you.

Next on this wonderful ridge was Nethermost Pike and like all the others this would be a magnificent mountain in its own right but is a little over shadowed by its bigger brothers. This one offers fabulous views of Ullswater. Sadly by now my knees were beginning to feel the worse for wear. Dollywaggon Pike has a lovely name but has a truly nasty descent down a scree slope to Grizedale Tarn. Both Kathryn and I were suffering somewhat by this time and my knees seemed to come to a grinding halt. The magazine I shared with Peter had advised me to bend my knees outwards, lean forwards and sway a little. Hence I descended looking a little like a cross between a chimpanzee and a troll. Kathryn who got a little impatient with the time I took and was still a little influenced by the ski lifts was traversing the slope from side to side and jumping 180 degrees with her feet together for each turn imitating a skier. Well it kept her quiet. Down by the tarn we both decided that Fairfield was beyond us both but compromised by deciding to still do Seat Sandal which was a delightful last hill before descending via Raise Beck. This provided a perfect end to a wonderful day and just to prove that every cloud has a silver lining, there at the bottom of the hill was my car, left there courtesy of Debby, hence we were saved the journey back to the quarry. Debby by the way was fine but has since avoided anything bigger than a hump back bridge.

The Six Minute Dash and Statues in the Snow

Kath and I were slumped on our sofa, mindlessly eating low fat biscuits, which are good because you can eat twice as many but bad because they taste so bloody awful that you need to finish off with a really decent chocolate digestive to take away the taste. We were discussing trivia. Derek, it being Saturday, was glued to the racing muttering incoherently at the screen, incomprehensible except for the repeated mantra, "if only," and "bloody jockeys."

It was the first of April and rather than get down to writing the reports for Key Stage Three, we were making up April Fool jokes to play on people. At least that was how it had started but in a very short space of time we had reached castration for one particular colleague. Not an April Fool in most people's book but this person deserved more than a gentle hoax. Derek, uncomfortable with the mention of castration and annoyed by the apparent sheer incompetence of his chosen jockeys and by our inane chatter, which prevented him really wallowing in misery, suggested that we go for a walk. After a long winter swathed in layers of home-knits, sitting in front of the fire and watching soap operas, at first this idea was about as attractive as childbirth in a third world field hospital. Derek, with a real flash of low cunning played his winning card, the only one he was to play that day as it later turned out. "If you're going to stay in then you may as well start those reports."

Kath and I, as one body, rose from the sofa with surprising agility given a) the sagging and worn out nature of our sofa and b) the sagging and worn out nature of our bodies. Anxious not to lose our new found enthusiasm, I suggested that we go and bag Fairfield, the crag we had missed on the last leg and which we really should get under our belts before crossing the road and tackling the next epic section. Kath went home to get changed and I went to scrape the mould off my walking boots that had been 'put away' at the end of last season. Once at the foot of Dunmail Raise, having spent the journey swapping fears of how unfit we felt and restraining Jacko who had realised

She started by striking explorer poses in the edges...

what was going on and had started throwing himself against the windows with glee, we stepped out into the crisp cold air.

We scrambled up the path adjacent to Raise Beck, shocked at how much of it had crumbled away in the winter frosts. This is one of my favourite sections of path in the whole of the Lake District, partly because I've been up or down it with so many of my favourite people and partly because it is so pretty. In fact I once took a group of children who were quite new to the countryside up it and when they had to write up a diary of their whole weekend it was the journey up this path that dominated their essays. Sometimes seeing something you take for granted through the eyes of others makes you appreciate them in a different way. I can more or less predict that at least three of those pupils will not get the chance to go onto the hills again and I'm glad that they got so much from this visit.

Today the beck was particularly beautiful as it was still festooned with icicles. Kath and I made a mental note to one day visit Iceland. The beauty distracted us from the pain in our limbs and lungs and we were soon at the half way point at Grizedale Tarn, laughing and loosening the layers of clothing as we steamed gently in the warming spring sunshine. Sometimes after a break from exercise your body seems to slip into gear in a way that is refreshing after the jaded feeling at the end of the previously busy season. We both felt alive and awake. It is of course always possible that after months of not being more than two feet above the ground, resting on a sofa, that we were suffering from altitude sickness but I don't think so.

There was yet more fun to be had though when Kath spied a left over patch of snow. There is something about a patch of snow in the sunshine that, when there is no one about to censure or tut, brings out the child in all of us. She started by striking explorer poses in the edges and was soon throwing herself bodily down into the snow to make body prints. We had a quick game of snowballs and built a snowman about which there could be no doubt of its gender but some doubt as to our sense of realism. We did have enough sense of dignity to modify it once we had stopped giggling, fearing to be the cause of heart attacks in the sort of tweedy old ladies I aspired to becoming. The dog bemused by being in the company of those more manic than himself, had withdrawn a safe distance and was lying low with his head between his paws.

Spring fever over we turned our attention to the scree path up Fairfield. I don't like scree as a rule but today we were in such high spirits that it didn't matter. We worked out that we had 40 minutes to get to the top and return to this point (not of course counting the stop at the top) if we were to stay on schedule. Off we went, scrabbling more often than not on our hands and knees, watching the clock all the way. We reached the top in 34 minutes. Jacko was in doggy heaven with all those cairns to scent-mark and it was a good job there were plenty of puddles to prevent imminent dehydration. Kath and I got out the thermos, the hip flask and the map and indulged in a bout of crag spotting, identifying those we had done and those we had yet to do. However it was too cold to linger and the shelter unlike the Des Res found on top of Glaramara, is not really worthy of the name.

Kath and I, always priding ourselves on our mathematical skills knew we had six minutes to get back to the tarn. We looked at each other and ran, ruck sacks and body parts bouncing, gasping for breath and still giggling, down the scree. We did it just in time and collapsed in a sweating heap for more cocoa, liberally laced with Amaretto. Kath, Jacko and myself were definitely back on tour!

Fence Posts In the Mist, 'Obvious Paths' and Looming Peaks

Lots of people moan about the weather in Cumbria but to be honest it's all part of the attraction. Without the rain there would be no lakes and after a heavy down pour the sight of streams tumbling hungrily down steep narrow gullies is breathtaking. There is nothing like being on the top of a peak in a high wind for blowing away the cobwebs of the nine-to-five drudge. The snow when it falls makes the hills magical and each step crunches when you walk like ice cubes dropped into gin. It is rarely slushy and hardly ever yellow. The sun when it shines is all the more welcome for its rarity and the Lakeland sun is clean and gentle not like the drowsy Prozac heat of the coast or the heavy dense heat that sends sticky sweat down the necks of the city boys in their shirt sleeves. It brings you out into blossom rather than sending you to sleep. Also it is capable of the most brilliant tricks of light. The Duddon Valley in autumn, for example, looks like someone has thrown a shower of new copper and bronze coins onto the trees.

Let us not forget the mist. I've once had the evening mists chase me down the fell as it crept upon me, quietly stalking me. The only other place I've experienced this creeping mist is on Dartmoor but there it feels a whole lot more threatening. Also most all-season walkers will have been walking all day in mist only for it to suddenly lift allowing them a quick but beautiful glimpse of the view. This experience is both reassuring and often stunning, especially as the image is frequently cloaked from view again in just a few seconds. Finally on a really wet cold grey day, when you've struggled up some fell in the mud it isn't half grand to sit in a Lakeland pub by a really big fire, listening to the rain, chatting to like-minded individuals and drinking Irish coffees.

Today we were intending to end the day with just such an experience. Kath's car had been deposited at the Dungeon Ghyll in Langdale and we were sat in mine below Dunmail Raise at the foot of Steel Fell. Dunmail was apparently the last king of

Cumberland but we didn't feel very regal at all. It was raining, misty and cold and the Irish coffees seemed a long way off.

Although we had picked the so called 'easier' route up Greenburn as our first choice, we were sorely tempted by the direct route which was only one mile long and kept more to the route followed by fell runners. Stupidly we changed our minds. Oh foolish maiden what have you done? This is a formidable wall of rock from whichever angle you approach it and as Wainwright says, 'The upper slope is quite as steep as it looks and there is no path to help.'

We began to follow the first of several fences we were to rely on that day. To say this is steep is an under statement. It is a vertical face capable of causing nosebleeds. I have never had so much opportunity to look backwards through my own knees at an upside down Seat Sandal. I felt like a Shetland pony in a rucksack. I swear at times I was not only on all fours, I was also hanging on with my teeth. Jacko, who started off on four legs didn't seem to notice and ran under the fence at will for the sheer joy of imagined trespass. Kath had turned magenta; I had gone beyond this and was indeed a whiter shade of pale by the time we reached the top. This is probably quite an impressive viewpoint but in the mist it seemed like a lot of effort for very little reward.

So it was without much of a break that we set off following another set of fence posts that gradually revealed themselves to us on our way to Calf Crag. This was not steep but was very, very wet. I actually think I developed trench foot on that stretch and Jacko showed signs of developing webbing between his toes. The mist got thicker and wetter, Kath and I got more despondent but Jacko loved it. He seemed delighted to roll in the foul smelling bogs then run up to us and shake himself. It's a bit of a strange feeling when so much depends on the sighting of the next soggy, broken old fence post. Odd how the mundane can be made vital by the vagaries of the weather. Eventually, after much wading and possibly even a little swim on Jacko's part, we arrived at Calf Crag. I have a theory about this crag. My navigation would get a 'could do better' if marked by a teacher yet, even in the mist and coming from any direction, I have always found this little hillock without error. I honestly believe that it emits some sort of subliminal chocolate smell or taste that draws me to it. I wish there were more fells like that.

Next on the agenda: High Raise, in theory. I say in theory because from here on in it all becomes a bit of muddle.

We found what we believed to be the ruined fence leading to the second cairn at White Stones. We passed a small tarn on our left, counted the requisite number of paces and turned due west. We were on flat ground and certainly very near the right spot but could find neither the large cairn nor the adjacent survey column. To paraphrase Oscar Wilde, 'To lose one landmark is unfortunate, to lose two...' You know the rest. We tried all the recognised methods of search. Enlarging the circle, quartering and our tried and tested favourite, wandering optimistically. We returned to the fence posts and got to the second cairn, took a bearing, counted the paces and... nothing, zilch, zero. To complicate matters there were by now several small tarns.

After twenty minutes we figured that we must have passed several times within feet of these land-marks but missed them in the mist (appropriate name for such a confusing weather phenomena). At any rate we believed that we had certainly been on the top and decided to head once again for those damned fence posts, and despite Wainwright's warning head for Sergeant Man. Visibility was by now literally three or four meters, we daren't get too far apart from each other and Jacko was most definitely on the lead. It's very unsettling when you inhabit a world made up entirely of middle aged, middle class art teacher, a sodden mongrel, yourself... and absolutely nothing else. Despite this fog, it had definitely gone beyond mist and was beginning to resemble Victorian London smog, we arrived without error at Sergeant Man.

The fells however had not yet finished being weird, far from it for out of the gloom wandered a very strange couple. They were probably between 40 and 50. She had on only a twin set and a pair of what my gran used to call slacks. She wore a pair of lace up Hush Puppies and had a little handbag over one elbow. Her blonde perm was immaculate. He had on a checked shirt, cords and a murky coloured cardigan with patches on the elbows and a zip up the front. He was not smoking a pipe but I'm willing to bet that he had one in his pocket. He was holding her elbow in that considerate way you rarely see these days. They had no map, no rucksacks and yet they didn't look at all weather worn. "The weather's coming in" I said. "We are going to get down as soon as possible."

"We've walked these fells for years," he said, "but today is particularly inclement." We tried to tactfully suggest that they came down with us but they just smiled and walked off together into the mist which quickly swallowed them up. Now this is not a ghost story and I don't really believe in such nonsense but this was a very, very peculiar encounter and, in the circumstances, down right unnerving.

We probably should have stuck to our guns at this point and gone down but we were on a mission and both the book and the map suggested that the route to Thunacar Knott was on 'obvious paths' with junctions marked by piles of boulders. Unfortunately what neither of them indicated was that that patch of the Lake District is possibly one of the most frequently visited and as such is literally riddled with 'obvious paths' and piles of boulders. The 'obvious path' that we were on was clearly not the 'obvious path' as it soon petered out to nothing. We tried following it back but must have gone wrong at one of the many junctions because the next 'obvious path' didn't even bother petering out, it just stopped.

After perhaps another twenty minutes of the headless chicken routine we did arrive at the shelter which is really not very far from our starting point of Sergeant Man. We were fed up, cold and wet so we stopped in the shelter for some Amaretto with a dash of hot chocolate and a Spar pork pie with apple on the top. We were just beginning to feel a little bit encouraged when there was a huge swooshing sound and the air in front of our faces moved towards us. This happened in a fraction of a second and, looking back it must have been a large raven or a buzzard swooping down just beyond our field of vision. At the very worst it could have been one of the Haweswater eagles that was either on an away day or had got lost in the mist. (Do birds do this and if not, why not?)

However to our tiny minds already rattled by the odd couple and the vanishing fells it could have been anything at all except something nice and gentle. We gave up on Thunacar Knott, although I'm fairly sure that we did cross it on one of our 'obvious paths' and decided instead to make for Pike o' Stickle, Harrison Stickle and Pavey Ark. Surely if we started from the shelter we couldn't miss those three.

The thing about the Langdale Pikes is that they are easily identified from any angle. They just cannot be anything but what they are. The fells, or tors as they are known, of the North Moor of Dartmoor are featureless and indistinguishable. This is what makes it such a great place to learn to navigate. The tops of the Pennines are, in my experience, largely a series of boggy, steep mounds. The Howgills are all smooth hemispheres, in fact there is a view from the M6 just before Tebay that looks just like a group of generously padded ladies all lying down and curled up in a sauna. It's all curves and creases. There are even some Lakeland fell tops whose summits beg the question "Are we here yet?" Purists in each region may disagree but one thing is certain, all would agree that the Langdale skyline, once seen, can never be mistaken for any other. Why then could we not find it? Because of this bloody mist, that's why.

After twenty minutes or so of wandering on more 'obvious paths' while also clinging as best as we could to a compass bearing we eventually arrived at Pavey Ark which we desperately tried to turn into Harrison Stickle. No mean feat when you know just how different these two are. Fortunately at this point we had our first stroke of luck for that day. A large gap appeared in the mist and there before us was the real Harrison Sickle. I tell you we ran as fast as we could and were well over half way there before the portal closed. This was enough however and we quickly reached our goal. Miraculously, the mists lifted once again and we hurried on to Pike o' Stickle. Having scrambled up to the top to what was our most certain peak of the day, I reflected on Derek's words when talking to Woodsy about his Bob Graham. He described the Langdales as an easy patch that was almost fun. Today the weather had made the familiar, for we'd both been up these hills several times before, very, very unfamiliar and had made the fun potentially very dangerous. I'd never before realised the value of broken fence posts, the treachery of 'obvious paths' or the beauty of looming hills. Next stop the pub!

The dog, bemused by being in the company of those more manic than himself, had withdrawn to a safe distance.

I calculate the amount of gear we carry with us in cardboard box loads.
Below - after another twenty minutes or so of the headless chicken routine, we did arrive at the shelter which is really not very far from our starting point.

There is something about a patch of snow in the sunshine...

A relentless and unremitting treadmill of turf clutching crawl...

The Great English Breakfast

I woke early and trust me 'waking up' is probably not the correct term, as I hadn't really achieved sleep. In order to get in my requisite number of camping nights for my Mountain Leadership certificate I had elected to camp in Langdale prior to this trip, the plan being that we would walk on two consecutive days. The rain was still drumming down on the tent, the ground sheet was clammy to say the least and I was cold in the way that you get when you get locked out at night and have to wait for someone else to get home to let you in. You know, when your whole body sort of shrugs in on itself and sets solid. Jacko was curled up, nose under his tail like an Arctic husky. He opened up one accusatory eye, glared at me and curled up even tighter. So much for Man's Best Friend. I tested my limbs to see if they really were as stiff as they felt, they were. I had a choice, I could drift into a doze and die of hypothermia, I could lie face down and face death by drowning (a bit of a slow option this, but at least it didn't involve getting out of the debatable comfort of the sleeping bag) or, if all else failed I could get up.

Eventually it was the smells emanating from Jacko's bottom that decided the issue. Some may view dog flatulence as a source of natural central heating and therefore welcome in the circumstances. I however, knowing Jacko well, recognise them as a signal that despite his apparent hibernation; he was due to be taken outside.

I fumbled around under the top of the sleeping bag and released the little gadget that keeps the drawstring in place. Prior to this only my nose had been exposed to the blasts of Baltic air. In retrospect this was probably not the best option given Jacko's contribution to the atmosphere of gloom. As the little opening became larger, gusts of cold damp air crawled in and wrapped themselves around any part of my body that had previously still believed that it would one day be warm again. Now was not the time to linger. I wriggled the top half of my body out into the air, the effort causing my breath to billow in damp clouds. It was then I remembered another reason why I hated camping - the feel of a wet tent. I have always imagined that if you pulled a week old corpse out of a slimy stagnant pond its skin would feel not dissimilar to the touch of a wet tent inner. Recoiling in horror I touched that other camp nasty, the wet ground sheet. I huddled up onto my sleeping bag and got dressed, contorting myself to avoid further contact with the sheets of slime. It was not a question of what should I wear. Layers were obviously called for so I simply found every dry article of clothing I had left and put it on over my night-clothes. This may have impeded movement but did make me a little less cold. Last on was my trusty waterproof, which for-tunately had been bought during a fat period and therefore, covered up all the other layers.

Jacko had now realised that it was time for the 'W' activity and in one swift movement, uncurled himself and hurled himself against the zip until it began to open. Then he scrabbled mole-like under the gap and made his bid for freedom, knocking over the last of the milk in the process. I followed in a slower but not much more dignified fashion. My god it was a monsoon! I quickly grabbed the essentials, then having swiftly pulled up the tent pegs, including the awkward one that wouldn't go in last night but was set in cement this morning, and without further ado bundled the whole lot into the back of the car. I would get everything out of the tent and fold it up properly later. Honest. Thank God for lightweight modern tents.

I now decamped to the toilet block and set up my Trangia. OK a loo is not the most hygienic of kitchens but, hey, what's cholera when you already have pneumonia, consumption and flu? Jacko, having now rustled the bacon everyone had left in the porch part of their tents and peed on several of the more expensive looking tents, returned to beg for his breakfast. The Trangia boiled and I let it bubble for a moment, so I could warm my hands in the steam. I sat miserably spooning in Readybrek made with powdered milk and drinking black tea. I swear the dog caught my eye and looked away sniggering before tucking into his own bowl of hot dog food. I was too fed up to wash up and simply threw all the utensils into the back of the car, which by now had come to resemble a rather smelly sauna.

Kath turned up much later amidst groups of irate campers

enquiring after missing food. Thank God the incessant rain had washed clean their tents. "Are we still going?" she asked.

"I suppose so," I muttered hoping that she wasn't keen.

"Oh good," she trilled, obviously refreshed after a night's sleep and a good breakfast. With my heart in my boots we set off for The Band.

This particular route takes you through a farm yard and no farm in Cumbria is without its cohort of farm dogs. There are usually at least two lean, mean looking collies, at least one of which has a wall eye out of which it glowers menacingly. Frequently these dogs are chained up and spend most of their time lying with their heads on their paws, willing an unwitting tourist to step within their accurately measured perimeters. Collies are by nature remarkably clever and to watch them work the sheep either at a show or on the fells is a treat. When chained up this intelligence becomes pure cunning and it is always best to give them a wide berth. Also roaming the yard are the inevitable terriers or possibly a Lancashire Healer. The latter are small very brave little dogs bred for rounding up cattle and are only rarely seen outside the north west. These terriers are nearly always ancient and cantankerous - even Jacko thinks twice before going into battle. Finally there is also often a large labrador, long since turned to fat, that just wants to put its head on your lap and cover you in drool.

We negotiated these hazards and passed through the farm under the insolent gaze of the farm cat. This was perched on the wall washing itself as if it hadn't even noticed you when in actual fact it could describe your every detail if it could be bothered to do so. By now we were both seriously wet.

"This rain," quipped the cheerful one, "is like Heineken."

"Because too much of it makes you sick?" I grumbled.

"No, because it reaches the parts that other rain doesn't."

"Ha bloody ha." Ten minutes later we were both literally soaked to the skin. Our clothes were wet and heavy and cold. My plan to wear lots of layers backfired and I was now carrying my own body weight in wet cloth. The wind pierced every layer and caused them to chafe uncomfortably. The mist obliterated everything beyond arms reach and the interminable path had become a grade four canoe course. Jacko's fur was plastered to his body and the rain dripped off his eye-lashes. He huddled close to our legs, trying to evade the wind.

"This is not fun," Kathryn shouted, turning to escape the wind. Relief flooded my body.

"Let's give up - well not exactly give up, just do the sensible thing, obviously only the foolish would continue." Thus justified, the three of us turned as one and body surfed back to the car.

"Do you know what I fancy?" I asked.

"Sean Bean and David Beckham in a big warm bed?"

"Tempting I agree but much, much better than that would be a real English breakfast."

Both our faces took on a look of rapture as we basked in private little dreams that appealed to every sense. Bean and Beckham eat your hearts (or in this case black puddings) out.

"Asda Calling," sang Kathryn to the tune of the old Clash song. "God bless Sunday opening."

Forty minutes later we were leaking round the said store leaving little puddles and steaming happily. Eggs, bacon - smoked and rindless, big firm beef tomatoes, tiny tightly curled pink and white button mushrooms, fat Cumberland sausages, baked beans, black pudding. Kath said she didn't like black pudding but I insisted they were part of the whole and could not be omitted. Hash browns, not sure what they are but, hey, why not? The basket full we strode past the dry croissants, the healthy yoghurts and the packets of gerbil food labelled muesli. It is not often the English can feel superior but when it comes to breakfast we truly are, 'A land of Hope and Glory.'

Back home we had a huge fry up, the smell of which tempted

even Derek down stairs and caused Jacko to drool uncontrol-
lably. Ten minutes later as we wiped great chunks of bread
across greasy plates, I finally felt warm and it was pure luxury
to slump into the sofa and watch the Eastenders omnibus.

Cut Paws, a Broken Car and The Testing of a New Love

It was on the New Year's Eve prior to this walk that Kath First met the 'Love Of Her Life,' Steve. At the end of a drunken night in Kendal, we all began to totter home. As we paused for one of our party to examine herself in a shop window, Kath reflected that she had really enjoyed talking to the little bald chap in the corner with an evil sense of humour. Janet and I needed little more encouragement. We ran cackling back to the pub. Unable to locate our quarry, we marched into the gents to the tune of hastily zipped up flies. Bumping into a very scared looking Steve, we then, in a most sophisticated way you understand, chorused, "our mate fancies you." We then scribbled Kath's phone number on his arm and ran out cackling and staggering. God are we a classy act or not? From this romantic beginning (Abelard and Heloise are not in this league) the rest is history. However at the time of this little trek the relationship was in its tender infancy, a fragile thing as yet uncertain.

The plan was to scurry up the Band, skip over the Crinkles and Bow Fell, hop over to Scafell Pike then bob up Scafell before returning to the Old Dungeon Ghyll in time for tea and scones. Those of you that can envisage this route will have spotted the very obvious flaw in our plan but hey, she was in love and I've always had a blind streak of optimism that borders on insanity. Of course the first point of call was the afore-mentioned hostelry where we readily imbibed, pausing only to greatly amuse ourselves at the expense of a dear friend Peter who was recovering (not sure on reflection that this is the right choice of word) from his stag night the previous evening. Suffice to say that no one was happy lighting up a cigarette within a four-yard circle of the said chap. Fortunately at this point we did a rare and strange thing, we looked at the map before we began. Thank God we did. By saying to ourselves, "well from there you may as well do this crag" and "from that point it would be a shame to miss this crag." We had talked ourselves into an epic. Now at this point sensible people shorten their route choice, but not us. Oh no. We just decided to alter our destination.

Kath who was still in that brief period of courtship when you can't say a sentence without using the loved one's name declared that she would ring Steve and ask him to pick us up in Wasdale. I have been married for long enough to know that such a request would be met with laughter at best and sheer bloody fury most of the time, was not convinced but off she trotted. She returned a few minutes later and said that she had left a message on the answer machine for him to pick us up at 6pm. Peter, through the fog of alcohol poisoning could spot the numerous flaws in this plan. Sadly he couldn't move his tongue sufficiently to verbalise them so off we pottered. Secure and happy as only idiots can be.

So here we were again, looking up at Bowfell. This crag had become a bit of a test for me. On the 15 October 1994 I had intended to do this top with my dad after we had been up Scafell. Scafell went well but on the way down my dad, who hadn't done much fell climbing at all, had begun to look tired. Suddenly for no reason at all he almost broke into a jog. He kept looking over his shoulder, frowning and speeding up. "Dad, for god's sake what is up?" I asked.

"Japs" he replied referring to the couple behind us. "Can't let them past." At this point I must explain that my dad is not really a racist. I know in every cell of my body that if a foreigner of any race was in trouble and he could help, he would. He has more integrity than any other person I know. However his dad died of pneumonia, believed to have been caused in the trenches, when my dad was ten. Also being raised in central Manchester my dad spent far too many days of his childhood in an Anderson shelter fearing for his life. Whilst I believe that he can forgive I know he finds it hard to forget. Therefore in any sporting event, Eurovisision song contest, Miss World pageant or it would seem fell walk he hated being beaten by the Germans or the Japanese. Anyhow we had a few choice words and I decided that we were not going to do Bowfell on that trip.

On the 2 November 1994 Kath and I had been rained off and retired to Asda (see previous chapter). On the 20 April 1995 we had attacked it from Rossett Gill but Kath began to feel very ill near the top of the gill and we only got back to the pub with the help of our emergency fig rolls having only bagged Rossett Pike that day.

To say I was optimistic, especially as we also intended to bag six other peaks before returning to a car in the next valley which may or may not turn up, probably gives you an idea of just how misplaced my optimism can be.

We set off up the Band and I adopted my usual emergency tactic. Andrew, Brian, Christopher, David, Edward. I finished boys' names just as my thorax lubrication system gave up the ghost and my whole throat turned into a sand paper wind tunnel. As I finished girls' names, my lungs exploded and I had a coughing fit saved only by flapjack and sweet tea. I moved onto cars. Thank God for the Zephyr and Xanadu. Finally when I had done places, animals and in desperation was about to start football teams we reached the top. The views were fabulous and it is one of those mountains that feel like you want a real mountain to feel. Majestic and inspiring. We felt a real sense of achievement. We quickly popped over to Crinkle Crags where we played at the count from Sesame Street. One crinkle, Two crinkle, et cetera. Childish I know but fun also. Then in front of us were the hills we were going to do and they looked fairly benign. Fools that we were.

There was only one other person on the top, a runner. We introduced ourselves and offered him some tea, which he took. He then told us that he was doing a back to back Bob Graham, ie. completing it one way then retracing his steps still in under 24 hours. In my opinion possibly Prozac and the number of the local Samaritan's group may, on reflection have been more use than tea but, each to his own. We chatted a little longer, after all we had plenty of time.

Next to fall under our boots and paws was Esk Pike. My log book entry reads as follows: "With Kath and Jacko as part 4 of our Bob Graham. A nice little fell that is really just an extension of Bowfell. From here it all looked so simple. If only we'd known." If only indeed! However this is a lovely crag and there were people to be chatted to, we duly chatted... and chatted... and chatted while Jacko scampered about begging and scavenging to his little heart's content. Then, exhausted by all that chatting we had a cup of tea and admired the view. Finally we set off for Great End, still innocently unaware.

Great End. Yes, this would have been a great end to this day's walking. Terrific views, more chatter, more tea, more begging (the later from Jacko you realise, Kath would not beg if she was down to her last shilling. Jacko has no such scruples). More chatter then a slow amble back down the hill. A Great End indeed but... Oh no, not for us, we were young, we were fit... we were stupid. Instead we admired at length the view of the Gables, as yet unconquered, then turned our toes towards the great Scafell Pike.

A quick carbohydrate-fuelled skip to Ill Crag and Broad Crag and then the big one. (Please note that Ill or Eel as part of a name means Evil. I tell you this benign little ledge had nothing of the head rotating, green projectile vomit inducing powers of its big brother). Scafell Pike is one of my favourite tops, it has views that are unsurpassed and gives a definite feeling of achievement. We celebrated this achievement with more chat, chocolate and coffee. (Why do so many nice things begin with the letter C? Cider, cuddles, cats, Christmas - the list is end-less and could perhaps one day provide a passable alternative to my alphabet game as a means of distraction from pain).

One more summit and weyhey, we were home and dry. The fact that we were a little late didn't initially worry us. In fact we spent a good twenty minutes at Mickledore watching an overly ambitious parent trying, it seems to lynch his reluctant offspring on Broad Stand. This is a popular spot with walkers who like to dabble in climbing and is frequently managed with the use of a safety rope. This chap had other more imaginative ideas. He had rigged up a makeshift climbing rope out of two ruck sacks attached together and strapped to the boy's body with his cagoule. I kid you not. The whole incident was a cliff hanger in every sense of the word. I'm glad to say it all ended well but obviously we couldn't move on until the boy had been lowered, albeit at times almost upside down. The father him-self had then performed a sort of inverted belly slide down this formidable obstacle. We had opted for the safer looking Lord's Rake which did sadly mean a considerable detour and some decent. We began the trudge   cream cakes, credit cards, climbers' bodies, champagne, curry - you see it works very well.

On arrival at the scramble Kath paled and began to bite her lower lip. Not a frequently seen gesture from the indomitable one who prided herself in her no nonsense, tweeds and bull dog mentality. "Have I mentioned my fear of heights?" she whispered, looking at her feet and turning her right heel outwards a few times. "Perhaps this is not the best time to mention it."

We got out the book and read the description. "Look," I said in my best 'cheery friend' voice, "three ups and two downs, how hard can this be?" Let me tell you how bad it can be. We more or less managed the scree slope before Jacko's ears were down and he took on a real hang dog expression. None of us liked the idea of going down before going up again, indeed Kath began to mutter about Stannah stair lifts but we had it to do so do it we did. The cross marked on the pinnacle to mark the deaths of four walkers was a really nice macabre touch and really lifted Kath's spirits, I don't think.

The final section proved too much for Jacko. He made a few attempts at scrabbling futilely up one of the bigger steps before sliding back down. At which point he sat down and howled. Kath also chose just this moment to have a panic attack of sorts and clung to the wall side with her finger and toe nails swearing and muttering curses. I scrambled down to try to retrieve Jacko but he was having none of it. He simply backed away under a rock and refused to budge. I tried everything. Coaxing, swearing, even tempting him out with the last piece of sandwich to no avail. If he was going to die it would be here, under this dammed rock and not out there on the slope of death. Suddenly from above we heard menacing tones shivering down towards us.

"Get that bloody dog out of there, get back up here and get me off this damned rock!" Jacko knows that Kath's wrath is to be feared more than simple death and he shot out ready to try again. Lifting him up each big step then hauling my own tired body up, we drew level with Kath. Jacko kept a respectful distance from her and gave her his most subservient look, I, if truth be told, did exactly the same. Slowly we encouraged each other up the slope, carrying a very subdued Jacko when necessary.

However it was not yet all over, oh no, there was still death by cairns to endure. A seemingly endless trail of little stone piles that mocked us as we entered the time warp that all tired walkers have known. It's like swimming through treacle. Time seems to both thicken and stretch as you plod onwards, ever onwards. I'm sure that by now some of the minor organs in my body had begun to temporarily shut down to enable my legs to drag themselves past each other with the monotony of school speech days. I could virtually feel my kidneys shouting, "Tools down lads, we're not putting up with this." After what seemed like the passing of a new ice age we reached the top and collapsed in the shelter.

It was only then that we looked at our watches and discovered that it was already six thirty.

"I am not going back down that bloody Rake," said Kath in a voice that was not to be trifled with. I also guessed that the two ruck sack and cagoule lowering system was out of the question. Sometimes you know, you just know that something is not even worth mentioning.

"You don't have to, we go by Foxes Tarn," I trilled. At this point we noticed that Jacko was doing this odd little body surfing manoeuvre which involved him lying on his belly and trying to raise all four feet off the floor. Was this some weird yoga pose to seek divine intervention? Was he stretching? Closer inspection however revealed that all four pads had cuts or grazes on them. He was obviously literally done for. The only way to get him down was to carry him and the only way to carry him was in a ruck sack. Have you ever tried to put a seriously pissed off Jack Russell into a ruck sack? I can safely confirm that it is difficult, very difficult, in fact very difficult indeed, but we did eventually manage to get him sat on lots of sweaters his head poking out of the top without actually suffering permanent loss of digits.

Walking when you're tired is laborious. Walking when you're tired and carrying a heavy ruck sack is horrendous. Walking when you're tired and carrying a heavy ruck sack with a two stone dog that wants to kill you is down right soul destroying. He would move one way then the other in a murderous attempt to bite my ears off. If he was pissed off before, he was giving his own little impersonation of the exorcist now. Things weren't helped by a passing tourist calling him cute and trying to pat his head. I never looked back but I'm fairly sure that that person's piano playing days are over.

We finally made it to the pub at eight o'clock to find Steve still waiting and relatively well tempered. Oh the blessing of new love. But fate had not finished with us yet. He actually greeted us with the phrase, "Well I never, two old bats and a dog well passed its sell by date." Yes I could have thought of several sarcastic replies but let's face it the last time I had met this man I was wielding a biro in the gents and also I was in no position to risk annoying him so instead I just forced out a laugh and said, "That would make a great title for a book."

At this point I would gladly have retired to the pub and drunk myself into oblivion but as Steve had already spent three hours of his valuable weekend in the pub I couldn't grumble when he led us towards his car. This car looked as if it had really seen life. I mean life had taken it by the scruff of the neck and shaken it into submission, its long and painful life story was writ large across its rusty little body but it was Steve's pride and joy. So risking life and limb for the fifth time that day, I crawled into the back and carefully released Jacko. At this point I have to say it was a good job that he was tired and an even better job that I was wearing thick gloves.

I quickly then did as I did in all risky situations, I fell asleep. I didn't care about dribbling, snoring or twitching. Steve wasn't my new boyfriend and he did look a tad put out to say the least. Kath, bless her, was so unctuously grateful, she even admired the car. Steve was slightly mollified and I sank deeper into sleep.

Thirty minutes later I became dimly aware that all was not well. I know very little about cars, in fact so long as the heater works, there's a radio and you can guarantee another 30 miles even though the petrol gauge is well below the red bit, I'm happy. I did know however that they are not supposed to smell like old fashioned tin kettles that have been allowed to boil dry for say, about a week. I knew that you weren't actually supposed to be able to hear the cogs and things under the bonnet grinding against each other and surely recently there had been a law about emitting clouds of worrying looking vapour from under the bonnet. I was also dimly aware that the landscape out of the window was tilted at about 45 degrees. Either the car was being winched up to auto heaven or we were on Hard Knott Pass.

In retrospect we should never have attempted to take that car up that road. I mean the Romans only built their fort half way up and to be honest this car could have remembered those days. For five long minutes we all silently willed the car onwards but it was futile. Eventually it didn't so much die as fade into submission. After all that rattling it all went very quiet and I half expected tumbleweeds to roll past in the way they did in old westerns.

Somehow we turned it round, I can't remember how. It seems to have been blocked out by my memory and will probably pop up in horrendous detail if I ever go into therapy. A worse shock was yet to come. The only alternative route, which avoided any significant hills, was via Ulpha and down onto the A590 under Windermere and onto Kendal. This is a journey I would hesitate to make if my sister needed a kidney and I had the only match. It is miles, in fact it must almost be a light year, definitely a light week at any rate and we had to make this journey at no more than 30 miles an hour in a car into which we had poured the contents of our water flasks. (How well do cars run on weak lemon squash?)

There was nothing for it. I went back to sleep. Every few hours I would raise my eyelids just enough to read the road signs. I tell you it was like the Tardis in reverse. Whole polar cycles elapsed. We were passed at least twice by birds flying south for the winter and back again the other way. And throughout all this Kath kept chatting pleasantly, keeping Steve sweet. She is truly a goddess amongst women and I can not praise her highly enough. Steve is waiting to be canonised.

The Missing Fell and the Amazing View

This was to be a bit of an expedition. It was the end of the summer holidays and we needed to blot out the misery of our return to school, probably even more than the children we were expected to teach, so we had planned an adventure. We would camp in Wasdale, complete the next leg of the Bob Graham, walk along the west coast peaks of the lake, take in an orienteering event and generally escape. We arrived on a lovely sunny evening and pitched my ancient Vango. I then got ready for the orienteering event, accompanied by the sound of Kath's scathing remarks. "You run up to a little flag, then you look for the next little flag and you run to that?"

"Yes."

How Kath makes silence sneer I will never know. I explained that 1) it was to help my navigation, (the sneering silence wrapped itself around me) and 2) I quite enjoyed it (the sneering silence rose up and tried to choke me).

I calculate the amount of gear we carry with us in cardboard box loads.

The event was one of those where you have to get as many checkpoints within one hour. I particularly enjoyed these as an hour is about the limit of this level of exertion I can cope with and there is absolutely no pressure to go on any longer, in fact quite the reverse.

The minute I left the starting box the superior one's attitude changed dramatically. "Run," she bawled, "Now." I realised in dismay that her competitive streak had kicked in only, sadly for me this was a case of competition by proxy. The first checkpoint was on a little island in the lake.

"I'll get my feet wet," I pointed out.

"Run," she bellowed and run, or at least paddle fast, I did. She clutched her copy of the little map with a fervour I have not seen before outside of my mother's Kendals sales forays in Manchester. "Run" she barked as she pointed up hill. I sloshed along already gasping and red.

"I want to get that one first," I pleaded, pointing to a point that was just about level with my current situation.

But oh no, "We'll get more if you go up first and then come down when you're knackered." I hadn't actually intended to get knackered or even mildly puffed out. My plan was to jog about on the lower level, picking off those at that level then gently amble back to the start, enjoying the evening before retiring to the pub. I don't have to tell you which plan we followed. I got my best score of the season and experienced wild hallucinations without the aid of any drugs whatsoever. It did cross my mind to join 'over ambitious friends anonymous' but I hadn't got the breath for the phone call.

I awoke next morning aching and stiff. Fortunately we had decided to do the West Bank fells on that day rather than tackle the big boys on the east. I won't go into detail. It is enough to say that Illgill Head and Whin Rigg are wonderful fell with high edges that you can sit on and dangle your legs over (if you have a death wish). Wastwater is the deepest of the lakes in the Lake District and the scree slopes are said to plunge below the water's surface for the same distance as they soar above it. Amazing. The boat house in the little wood at the end is idyllic and the long arduous scramble over the boulders of the screes was an adventure not to be missed (except possibly by Jack Russells who do find it a bit of a challenge).

On our way back to camp we visited the tiny chapel by the valley head. This is a spot often missed by tourists but is one of the district's real gems. Like something out of a Hardy novel it stands, smaller than most people's houses. The graves of local climbers in the little cemetery are a poignant reminder that fell sports are not without risk but that for some people, the love of the fells will drive them on whatever the risk.

Once back in camp we realised that we had some neighbours. A group of young lads were flicking up one of those modern tents that seem to almost self assemble. "Hello girls, nice to meet you, to meet you nice," the taller one called out. I instinctively looked over my shoulder to see whom he was addressing. Once you reach a certain age you are not often referred to as 'girl' except by very old men of dubious intention. To be called thus by one who still bore the traces of cradle cap was bemusing to say the least. Realising that he did mean me, I had the choice on one of two options. I could giggle coyly like a sad middle aged Barbie or I could make a confused sort of greeting that was most likely to convince someone that I was in fact slightly addled. I chose the latter but it didn't matter, as it soon became clear that the conversational input required on my behalf was minimal. Within about two minutes they had introduced themselves, given us their life histories and explained that they were a group of sixth form army cadets from Essex who were preparing for their Gold Duke of Edinburgh. I quickly grasped that I was supposed to be inordinately impressed by each part of this explanation and tried to smile appreciatively before wandering over to our tent. There was something about these lads that I just didn't get.

We quickly got changed inside the tent, well put on new socks anyway, and emerged ready for a swift cup of tea and several chocolate digestives while we waited for the pub to open so we could get our evening meal. The outside of our tent was soon spread with boxes, deck chairs, coats, the dog's accoutrements and of course socks hanging off the guy ropes. The cadets on the other hand had all their boots in a neat line and one lad was ardently rubbing in dubbin (was it January already?). Another was constructing some sort of kitchen unit/pan stand thing from fallen branches lashed together with boot laces while the other two were effortlessly cooking what appeared to be a five course meal on the smallest gas cooker I have ever seen. After watching me fiddle with the trangia for a few minutes they gave us both a cup of Earl Grey and asked us what we were having for tea.

"Oh the stove, that's just to make a brew. We're going to eat in the pub." They gave me back the 'Does not compute' look I had given them earlier. We enjoyed the tea and chatted for a while. They explained that they were so determined to keep the weight of their packs down that they had actually drilled holes into the handles of their cutlery. They each proudly told me the weight of their packs in kilograms point grams. Sadly this failed to impress me as I'm not yet 100% metric though I've nearly cracked decimalisation and anyway I calculate the amount of gear we carry with us in cardboard box loads. Again the look flashed between us. Kath and I finished our tea and left them to it. We secured a mutinous Jacko in the car and retired to the pub for hot steak and kidney pie followed by treacle sponge and a few gins.

That night an evil storm blew up and we awoke to hear the ten flapping. Jacko had huddled inside my Buffalo jacket and was looking mournful while the sky emptied itself over our field. Kath and I shivered inside our respective bags listening to the thunder and wind. We both knew that we had to get out and deal with the flapping fly sheet but were both hoping that lightning would actually kill us first making this option unnecessary.

Eventually after a particularly nasty gust of wind drove one side of the roof almost to the floor we realised that we had no choice. We both got up and put on our wellies. Once outside we began to knock back in all the tent pegs that had been literally wrenched out of the ground. Other campers, including the cadets were doing the same. Suddenly it all became clear. The cadets were wearing large waterproof capes, strong boots and hats; they were knocking in their pegs, which all matched with purpose-built mallets. I had on wellies and my Snoopy pyjamas over which I had pulled my large waterproof, which was somehow inside out. My hair was blowing in all directions but mainly into my eyes and I was knocking in an odd assortment of pegs gleaned from tents now dead. Furthermore I was using a walking boot as a mallet while Kath hammered away with a baked bean tin. Quite simply there was nothing wrong with the cadets or indeed with us. We were just from two different worlds, possibly even two different species and communication was never really going to occur.

We arose early, faintly glad to still be a) alive, b) dry and c) in more or less the same spot that we had been before. Kath and I had a hearty breakfast while the cadets went through a series of Swiss army exercises, which confirmed my thoughts from last night. I tell you no one should be able to do that with their legs. It made us so tired we finished off the bacon and had another cup of tea. They were going to do the same route as us but in reverse order. This, apparently, was so that they could go up the mighty Kirk on the direct route. They said that this would be an excellent challenge. Wainwright himself describes it as being, 'A relentless and unremitting treadmill of a turf- clutching crawl' with 'Only three opportunities for standing upright.' 'Challenge' is not the word I would choose.

Kath and I set off back down the road, (on which you can stand upright any time you wish). We agreed that yes the fell we were approaching did indeed look like an up turned boat. We reached Overbeck Bridge in the sort of clearer than normal sunshine that often follows a heavy down pour. As always we were puffed after the first hundred yards or so of ascent before second wind takes over. We mused on two things. Firstly is this period of fatigue in fact your body's way of telling you, 'No don't do it, you could be on a sofa somewhere' and secondly did fell runners have a secret capacity to achieve third or even fourth winds? The conversation took a predictable low turn at that point but at least it got us both up the side of the wall and as such well on our way.

Jacko being one of nature's deviants had taken the opportunity of being unobserved to find his own amusement. He had found a huge bone which was probably a limb from a dead sheep but which could easily have passed for the hip bone of a buffalo. Not only was this bone huge but it was gruesome and very, very smelly. In fact it still had the bedraggled remnants of fur and flesh hanging off it and it had certainly been dead for a long, long time. Jacko was in ecstasy. He had first rolled over and over on top of his macabre trophy, ensuring that his smell and the rotting corpse's smell were now indistinguishable and was now gnawing it with relish. Every now and again he would try to give it a vigorous shake to ensure that it was indeed dead. God knows why as the stench was ample evidence of this fact. Every time we tried to take it from him he would throw back his head so that it rested on his shoulders in order to lift the thing up and gallop off with it. As he couldn't actually see in this position, his progress was hazardous and we decided that distraction was the answer.

We reached the turn in the wall and took the path left. There was no way I was going up Bell Rib with a person who is nervous on ledges and a psychotic dog who keeps running into things because he has his own personal comfort corpse. It was time for a break so we looked for a suitable spot. On reaching the west face of this mountain we were greeted with one of the several fabulous views that we were to be granted that day. Overbeck was in full and turbulent spate after the rain the night before and along with its tributaries it was tumbling down massive gullies that looked as if they had been clawed out of the hill side by a huge talon. The waterfall was a surging mass of white foam. This was the place to rest.

We set about trying to distract Jacko from his ghoulish trophy. This is usually an easy task as Jacko's memory span makes the average goldfish look like a MENSA candidate. Indeed I have often been tempted to write the word 'Breathe' next to his basket just in case one morning he forgets. Today was different however. No amount of rustling crisp packets, proffered digestive biscuits or even Kath's fresh swordfish with French mustard and a rocket salad on ciabatta (I ask you) could tempt him away. It seemed that he had gone feral. He would drag this thing out of our reach then gnaw on it ravenously, pausing only to howl like a horror story wolf. The sight of this gore stained mis-shape devouring a corpse and howling was drawing looks of pure disgust, and at times naked fear from picnickers. To paraphrase Margaret Thatcher, who deserved the fate intended for the Christopher Fry character in the book that she herself was paraphrasing, 'The dog was not for learning.'

Embarrassed we moved onwards towards the scramble at the top of this route. Faced with this rocky path, Jacko remained determined to cling to his bone and began to drag it up the rocks. I attacked the scramble with enthusiasm, pretending that Jacko was not mine and tutting along with passers by at his ridiculous behaviour. Kath often does this to me so I didn't feel guilty at all.

Suddenly I passed between two large upright pillars and was faced with... nothing, just a sheer drop into an abyss. I had reached Great Door and was treated to the second spectacular view of this trip. Jacko, by now panting for breath, scurried onto the ridge and tried to stop. Unfortunately the corpse was adding to his momentum and for a moment he teetered on the brink. My heart went out to him, it really did. After carrying his prize up the mountain he was faced with the choice to either let it go over the edge or die with it. With great sadness he opened his jaws and the thing tumbled over the edge to be lost forever. Bereft, Jacko sank to his belly and put his head on his paws. Briefly, he had lost the meaning to life. This was soon restored however when a kindly fellow traveller who had witnessed the whole event gave him a real dog biscuit. Jacko has never been given such treats and almost gave himself up for adoption on the spot.

We circumnavigated the Door and arrived at a very pleasant summit. One down, four to go. The route to Red Pike was a long trudge, not difficult, just long. In fact do you know the song Climb up Sunshine Mountain? Well take away the sunshine and there you have it. Mental and physical exhaustion could possibly be used as an excuse therefore for the sheer stupidity that was to follow. We never found the Chair, to be honest we didn't look very hard, but we did eventually reach the summit. Here we stopped for a snack. I attacked a black pudding butty while Kath nibbled daintily on a Cajun chicken wrap. Jacko wasn't fussy and happily guzzled up scraps from both culinary delights. After a couple of Spar cakes (made in the Sandylands Spar and huge bricks of delicious sticky calories) and a mug each of hot chocolate laced with Amaretto from my hip flask we got out the map and tried to plot our route.

We could see both Great Scoat and Little Scoat Fells and ok, yes, I admit it, we made the obvious schoolboy jokes before looking further. I blame the Amaretto. We could also see Pillar and Kirk but where the hell was Steeple. OK I know that any one reading this who is only slightly brighter than my dog knows the answer and is already laughing scornfully but as I said we were tired and Amaretto can play funny tricks on your mind. Time and time again we checked it out with a compass to no avail. It wasn't there. We pondered as to whether it had been sold to the Americans like Tower Bridge or if it had been moved. Worse still when we looked at the Principle Fells diagram in the guidebook it didn't exist here either, yet there it was clearly marked on the map. Where was our missing fell? Now both Kath and I have degrees, OK they are not firsts in Geography or Advanced Mathematics but we don't consider ourselves to be thick. Imagine our humiliation (I'm cringing while I'm writing this) when after a good five minutes head scratching it finally dawned on us. Great Scoat is 2760 foot high and according to our map this is paradoxically even smaller than Little Scoat. Both of them stood in front of Steeple which is only 2687 foot high. Of course we couldn't see the bloody thing, its bigger neighbours hid it from view. Der!

Embarrassed, we made our way quickly to Little Scoat, followed by a wall of fine mist which overtook us just as we arrived. Great, here we go again. This time the mist however added to the magical mystery that had become our journey to the hidden fell. We walked into a patch of cloud and faithfully followed a wall to... a patch of cloud. We followed a line of cairns as directed through... a patch of cloud. We crossed a dramatic arete that felt like the Carrick a Reed bridge with walls of mist descending steeply on either side and arrived at... a patch of cloud. What a brilliant summit, it was like being on a tiny magic carpet, just a cairn a patch of grass and a sea of mist. Kath said she kept expecting to see trolls. Perversely, we couldn't have reached this top in better conditions.

Two fells to go. The journey from Steeple to Pillar involves a lovely ridge walk, which has a slight scramble after Wind Gap but is really just a promenade. Real Bob Grahamers will probably disagree. The mist floated on past us and away over Buttermere, leaving us with a perfect evening view. One thing we did decide was that we would be leaving Kirk until the following day. It looked huge, and we were tired. Unlike fell runners, we don't push on through when we hit 'The Wall.' We looked for a stile and used it as a seat while we enjoyed a snack.

Pillar itself was beautiful but fairly unremarkable. It was here however that we met up with the cadets who it seemed had been on the Buttermere round with extras. The one to whom I had spoken most approached me. Standing on that fell in the crisp pink sunset of a late summer evening he said, "Brilliant here isn't it?"

I tell you it was like ET's glowing finger or that strange little tune in Close Encounters. Somehow two completely alien beings had found a point of communication.

"Yes," I agreed, "absolutely marvellous." We both smiled and went our separate ways.

Kath, Jacko and I wound our way back to camp down Mosedale Beck, not once regretting not having climbed Kirk; it would save until tomorrow. The following day however brought more torrential rain so we changed our plans and visited Sellafield instead. I wish we hadn't. At the end of the visit I felt that I had learned only what they wanted me to learn and seen only what they wanted me to see. I had the distinct feeling that Kirk Fell in the pouring rain was a place a million times more acceptable than this.

We never did do Kirk that trip but it had been a very varied visit with lots to commend it. It still remains my favourite valley and I'm glad we went.

Guest Houses we have Loved

It had been a bad week at work, particularly bad. It was May 1996. There had been the letter from OFSTED and management had gone into paperwork overdrive. Basically it had become a case of if it moves record it's progress, if it doesn't move write a policy document, a risk assessment and an objectives forecast for it. The children had picked up on the fact that some staff were already off with stress, and those that were left were slumped over word processors, gibbering. Ours were not the type of children to happily cope with prolonged periods of silent reading and chaos had broken out in several places. Kath, as the art teacher, had been prodded into producing displays, which were to outdo the Uffizi in both quantity and quality. I had had several cover lessons and in desperation had resorted to chocolate microwave meringues, popular with the children but a bugger to clean up after.

By Friday break we needed respite care and were desperate to escape to the hills. We decided to drive round and bag our missing fell, Kirk. This would be a long drive and rather than try to endure it in the morning, we both decided that we had to put as much ground as possible between school and ourselves.

We had been back to tick off Grey Knotts, Brandreth and both Gables on a fairly uneventful trip, which is never the less worthy of a paragraph or two, though not a whole chapter. We had parked again in the Honister car park, Kath actually took my keys off me and physically pushed them into my Buffalo front pocket before zipping it up forcefully in a manner I've only ever seen before in Oliver Hardy. It's not my fault that I lose keys like Kylie loses weight.

We opted to follow the fence post route, which is very steep but easy and fast, and as result it didn't take too long to get to the summit. However as soon as we got there a phenomenon, which you never see in towns occurred. A thick mist seemed to just drop out of the sky, everything went dangerously quiet and that was it. We could barely see each other. Jacko, sensing that he may become genuinely lost as opposed to just hiding to make a nuisance of himself, cowered in close against our legs. This fog didn't drift or swirl it just sat and grew thicker. We had a map and compass and I was eager to continue. We studied the map and the guidebook, which included the rather worrying signpost for 'sudden death', worked out the pacing and strode off into the unknown.

I kept expecting to meet Captain Kirk or Doctor Who but in fact we arrived at the scrap heap that marks the top of Brandreth with no problem at all. Spurred on with this success we moved onto Green Gable. Inspired by glimpses of stunning tops and valleys which were momentarily shown to us when we passed through pockets in the mist before again being blotted out we got there and made good use of the shelter. Our compass seemed to urge us lemming like over a precipice but the path makes a grand prix turn and we got to Gable via the back door. Everyone raves about this peak and it had caused great awe in us from several angles. We had been looking forward to seeing it. We were disappointed therefore to travel that entire way and barely even see the summit. Indeed we searched at length for the plaque only to give up and then sit on the damned thing. At this point we erred on the side of caution and decided yet again that Kirk could wait.

Getting back was weird, the wandering around on the top had disorientated me completely and I didn't want to follow the compass at all. This is a horrible dilemma faced at some time by most walkers. You try to make excuses for the compass. My favourite is iron deposits in the soil. Thankfully I was with Kath, who struggles to use a compass, but has an amazing sense of direction. I swear she is part homing pigeon.

"It's this way," she stated and set off almost in line with the compass. We got back safely, me relying on the compass, Kath inexplicably drawn back to her fridge and sofa. She gives a whole new meaning to the term 'Fridge magnet'. Yet until we got back to Brandreth I was completely convinced that we were heading in entirely the wrong direction. This leap in faith in your compass is very scary yet very necessary and I hope that I don't have to make it too often.

But back here on the coast road we drove on towards Kirk. Yes it was raining, yes the forecast was for worse but we blithely told ourselves that it would clear, such was the urgency of our need to get away from work and to finally get this bloody mountain under our belts. The coast road is long in daylight, but in torrential rain in the dark it goes on forever.

At first we were optimistic, then we were unnaturally jolly, making jokes about the fact that there is never an ark available when you need one etc. However by Muncaster, we realised two things. One: we had come too far to turn back to Kendal and Two: even if we could get the tent up in the hurricane currently battering the window, it probably wouldn't stay up and even if it did we didn't want to spend the night inside it. What would fell runners have done? we mused. "Well the real tough ones would probably be already hunkered down inside a large orange polythene bag or wrapped themselves up in a tin foil sheet," Kath suggested without enthusiasm.

"What about the softies?" I asked.

"No such thing," she replied. "At the very least they would pull the car over and sleep in that," she added. We both looked around my car, strewn with discarded crisp packets and petrol receipts, plastered in dog hairs and mud and with 2cm of dirty water sloshing around our feet.

"Yes but we are fell walkers, not fell runners and what we lack in muscle and stamina we make up for in common sense," I declared.

"Yes, that is why we set off to go camping in a deluge," Ms Sarcasm muttered. Not deterred I pulled up in a lay by.

"I'm not sleeping in this vehicle with that dog," she says all hoity toity. I resisted the urge to tell her that if anyone was leaving it wasn't Jacko. After five minutes rummaging in my well-packed ruck sack, discarding the sun screen, more empty crisp packets, a packet of American Tan tights (No, I don't know either) and a large orange polythene bag I found the only sort of plastic emergency gadget that never fails. Clutching my credit card and hoping that when they ran it through their machine I wouldn't hear sirens and bells and that an iron cage would not drop from the ceiling and imprison me while police cars pulled up in droves, I rang the bell of the guest house.

Somewhere in the bowels of the building a bell rang and, several minutes later, a rather gaunt gentleman put his head around the door. I've always been a bit of a rocky horror fan and, just for a brief second I wished I was in a basque and suspenders.

"Yes," he said. I never knew it was possible to get so many syllables into such a small word.

"Do you have a vacancy, a double?" I asked.

"Yes," again, said in a tone that gave nothing away.

"Do you take visa?"

"Yes," ok that was two out of three but the next one would surely blow this deal out of the water.

"Do you take dogs, he is very small and quiet and house trained?" I gasped the words tumbling out.

"Yes." Bingo...!

We were shown into the warmest, cleanest, most comfortable room I've ever sat in while our room was made ready. I caught site of our reflection in a perfectly polished mirror. Two soaking wet women with hair plastered to white faces, me with my work a day make up smeared across my cheek because I'd been in too much of a hurry to remove it. Standing in this pristine haven, we were both dressed in the layers of old jumpers that we used for walking in, and Jacko, muddy to his knees, was straining at the end of his leash and snarling at a cat which was hidden under a chair. He didn't look small, quiet or house trained; in fact he didn't much resemble a dog. More your average Gremlin if truth be told. Yet this man showed us to a lovely clean room, offered us coffee and cake (Kath at this point took on the expression I'd only ever seen her use before on Valentine's night after several quarts of gin - I was certain that she was ready to swear her undying devotion). The beds were firm and clean with those thick, crisp white sheets you only find in hospitals or posh hotels. I slept like Rip Van Winkle and dreamed, oddly, of eating lemon cake and drinking tea from a china cup in Lewis's tea room.

In the morning we got up early, ate a delicious breakfast, continued our journey and climbed up Kirk Fell. It was a bit of a monster with a string of at least five hundred little cairns leading to a very dull summit and we did have a bit of a moment on the ascent but we did it. If this book is ever read by anyone other than immediate family and this guest house gets any business from it, then my efforts on the word processor will not have been in vain. This man and his lovely home deserve a medal. As for fell runners, well you see guys, why run for 24 hours when you can sleep in a warm bed for eight!

Paradise on Earth and the Saving of a Beautiful Friendship

It was a bit of an occasion, we both agreed as I parked my mini in the car park at the top of Honister Pass by the youth hostel. We were on the final three peaks of our own personal Bob Graham Round. After this it was just one more trip from the top of Dale Head back to Keswick. A purist would have put the two together but, as always real life has a nasty habit of intervening and, even though it was the end of August and a beautiful day we both had mundane but necessary little tasks calling us in from the hills.

The plan was to leave my car at the top of Honister Pass and drive down to the Fish in Kath's car thus avoiding having to walk on the road. I locked the mini and carefully placed my keys in my pocket, smugly congratulating myself on remembering that I would need them later. We then got into Kath's car and drove down to the Fish to park there. I removed the keys carefully from my pocket and tucked them under the rubber mat in Kath's car, again congratulating myself on a rare moment of security. I know, I know, I know... now.

I'm quite fond of this hostelry, partly because I love the novel The Maid of Buttermere but also because, in my opinion it serves the biggest portions of well cooked food this side of my favourite chippy in Plymouth. They are huge and great value for money. Food was, unusually, not really on the agenda today although we did both tuck into ice creams and mugs of tea but everyone knows that food eaten outdoors doesn't really count anymore than free nibbles in supermarkets or anything with lettuce in it. We sat for about ten minutes discussing the futility of the working week. Three days on and four off would solve unemployment, and if done on a rolling basis remove the idea of a weekend which puts most people under pressure to have fun. This is impossible as basically they are knackered and anyway they have only two days to do the chores, visit family and maintain the house. Some break! Mind you five days off and two on sounded even better. Better still very early retirement.

Having thus set the world to rights we set off up the side of

Robinson. OK so we were doing these crags in reverse but by now deviation had become the norm.

We set off up the gentle path on the soft grass nibbled to resemble a green skinhead, by sheep that looked like walking rugs. The bracken patches had not yet begun to rust and had not yet begun to uncurl upwards to meet the sun. We got to the top of this impressive crag no problem. The summit was unusually silent apart from the occasional 'prook prook' calls of the wheeling ravens. The huge fells on the other side of the valley tumbled down into the lake, which shimmered in the weak sunlight like the skin on the dog's back when he shivers. I felt as if I had been given a psychic massage and that my soul had been eased gently back into alignment with something bigger, older and wiser than myself. In short I felt at one with myself and a small part of a greater whole. Walking can sometimes do this and at that moment I felt blissful. We could see a lot of the bigger peaks that we would still have to tackle another day but today's challenge seemed a pleasant one indeed.

Hindscarth was next to fall under our feet. Yes, it involved some effort but nothing too strenuous and we spent some time chatting while sitting on the unremarkable but pleasant summit. I lay back on the soft grass and closed my eyes in the gentle sun. One more crag to go then an easy drive back up the valley. Oh my God! My body tensed like it had been electrocuted.

Bugger, bugger, bugger, I was about to die. The keys to my car were the keys I had so carefully hidden under the mat in Kath's car; the keys I felt so smug about being diligent about. The keys I would need to start my car in order to drive it back to Kath's car. Shit she was going to kill me.

Dale Head loomed and all my joi de vie had left to be replaced by an ocean of tea and ice cream trying, like rats to leave the doomed vessel. I tried to remain jolly while all the time racking my brains for a cunning plan. Why hadn't I paid closer attention to my students as they described to new pupils how to hot wire cars. I had learned from them that, allegedly you can break into a car using half a tennis ball but where on the fells was I going to find such an object? Also I had a sneaking feeling that this only worked on cars with central locking systems and as I was unclear what exactly this meant I wasn't sure whether I had it or not.

"Do you know," I sang, "I could walk for ever today."

"Really, I'm beginning to fade myself," Kath said. She looked down the steep slope into the valley. "When we were driving it didn't seem that far, it's quite a long way really>"

"True but it is down hill."

Kath gave me her best Gestapo, 'Is there something you're trying to tell me?' look which has wormed some terrible secrets out of big tough sixteen year old street children. Inside I quaked but I also work with these adolescent rottweillers and had almost certainly learned more from them than they had from me so I smiled beatifically and pointed to the sky away to our left. Is that a sparrow hawk?

The beautiful views on the top of Dale Head were wasted on me. My usually vivid imagination and strong sense of self-preservation had given up on me. Taking advantage of Kath's cheerfulness caused by this being technically our last fell, I confessed all. To be fair she took it very well although this view was not shared by a German family who covered their children's ears and scurried down the path. Even Jacko put his tail momentarily between his legs until for him both the moment and the memory were lost forever, ie. thirty seconds.

"You ll just have to hitch a lift," she growled. Prior to this I don't think Kath had ever hitched a lift, it has to be a dire emergency before she will get on a bus. For her, public transport means taxis. However I had hitched from Ilkley to Northampton regularly while at college and I knew that certain things were not beneficial when trying to get a lift. Top of this list were scruffy grubby clothes, huge rucksacks and, a total no no for hitching - a dog.

It was with very limited enthusiasm then that I put out my thumb when we heard an approaching engine. I didn't even look over my shoulder as I was still casting my eyes down in the manner of some eastern supplicant who fears that public stoning is not far away. However the engine slowed and I looked up to see a tiny Birkett's grocery delivery van parked up just ahead. I ran to the door and burst into my best distressed damsel routine.

"Nay lass, don't you worry, you just hop in the back and I'll get you to the pub." Kath and I didn't need telling twice and we scrambled into... an absolute paradise. There were tins and garden produce against one wall but facing us was a tray of fresh cream cakes. Jacko, or possibly Kath but I like to hope not, began to whine piteously and I could not distract him with a tin of kidney beans.

"I have a few calls to make before the pub so if you're hungry just help yourself, give the little hound a bite too." I swear I heard a rendition of the Hallelujah Chorus.

Kath had a vanilla slice, I had an elephant's foot and Jacko had a cream scone. As we all licked the cream from around our lips, our new friend explained that he delivered to all the remote homes and farms in the valley and that what he didn't sell would only get thrown away. Kath, always open to opportunity asked if he was thinking of retiring soon and did he think they would employ her if he did so. He went on to tell us a great deal of local history and kept us very entertained. We were sorry to get to the Fish and reluctantly climbed out of the little van. A great tragedy had been avoided, we had climbed all our peaks and we had had cream cakes. It had been an excellent trip.

Two Against The Clock

We had been adding up all the time we had taken to do each leg, allowing for getting to the starting point, doing extra peaks et cetera and also taking in the time spent stopping to chat (An alarming amount which I'm not prepared to print). Although the whole thing had taken two years and six months, it was still possible that we could finish with an actual walking time of 48 hours and this was today's goal. We were taking a variation on the original theme but then by now this should come as no surprise at all. After all how many real Bob Grahamers would have included Sergeant's Man twice and paid a visit to Scoat Fell just because they took a fancy to the name? In order to bag three more Wainwrights, we picked a route that included Catbells, High Spy and Maiden Moor. It's a similar distance so we reckoned that it wasn't really cheating. We had first to climb Dale Head again so that we could start the clock at the top which was irksome to say the least but was relatively soon out of the way and we started up the stopwatch.

In the clear blue sunshine we set off back down the hill we had just climbed, this time heading due west towards Dalehead Tarn, thus circumnavigating the other Great Gable. Surely the first is stunning enough or so we'd been told. Why have two? Having said that though both Kath and I are definite witnesses to the fact that mountains can get lost so perhaps it is as well to have a spare. Today this sort of incident was not going to be a problem, we could see the little tarn right from the word go so even we couldn't really miss it. On arrival we turned north and there in front of us was High Spy. Easy peasy. So relieved of the burden of navigation, we fell into conversation. This bit was reasonably flat so it was one of the rare occasions on this route where we could both talk and breathe without risking asphyxiation.

Somehow we got onto the subject of amateur dramatics. Kath's whole life is like a Rogers and Hammerstein production as she never stops performing to the crowd and is always an entertainer, starring in each role that she adopts. I have also had my moments and it was one of these I related to Kath now. It was the third High Lane Brownies and Cubs Christmas nativity play and I was desperate to be an angel. I already knew all the lines and had made my own halo in November, slightly modifying the Blue Peter coat hanger candle thing. If ever there was an angel in waiting, I was it. However back in the late 1960s there was no such thing as political correctness and only blonde beautiful children could be angels. I was too short to play Mary and the cubs were allocated all the roles of wise men. (God only knew why, our cub troop was not gifted in any way at all. Not that I'm bitter of course).

Brown Owl's twins were allocated the shepherds and Akela's lad was the innkeeper. That left four of us. Me with my fuzzy red mop and freckles, a kid with a lazy eye who had glasses with one eye blacked out with elastoplast, the fat kid and what would now be called an 'academically-challenged' kid. We were given the rather non specific roles as animals around the crib. Specky's mum made her a camel, rather cruel, as a hump as well as a lazy eye did nothing for the innate desire we all had to look like Barbie. Fatty was made into a donkey with the addition of a cardboard mask and an old rug and Dopey was dressed in an inside out sheepskin coat that belonged to her dad and another mask that was supposed to complete her transformation into a sheep. My mum however surpassed herself. She had an old roll of black lining fabric and set to work on my costume. Throughout rehearsals much was made of the angels, kings and the family and we were just instructed to mill about quietly. We never had a dress rehearsal.

Come the glorious evening all our parents were sat steaming in the village hall waiting for curtain up. Everybody had to stay on stage for the whole time and only move forwards when it was their bit, there was no back stage. The four of us were huddled near the back corner almost out of sight. The angels and shepherds did their bit then the Kings, one of whom was I remember very reluctant to give up his gift. Finally it was our bit; we shuffled towards the crib and then, my finest moment. I lifted my head and raised my arms to reveal my character......the Christmas bat!

I had a brilliant batman hood and huge wings, which I held the tip of in my tightly clenched fists. There was a stunned gasp in the audience then my mum began to cheer. Urged on by this I began to flap wildly and make loud squeals, which I felt appropriate to a bat. I was spectacular! Realising that it was now or never, our troop went wild. The donkey reared up and whinnied, waving its coconut shell hooves menacingly over the crib, the sheep bleated like she was being slaughtered and threw hay about and the camel went ballistic running around the stage, by now totally unable to see with her one good eye as her mask had slipped. I continued to raise my wings over the Tiny Tears doll that was supposed to represent Christ and I added the odd squeal for good measure. Two of the angels fled in tears. Yes! angels nil, numpties two. Mary stuck her thumb resolutely into her mouth and backed away. Order was only restored when our infant teacher who was doubling as the narrator, strode on stage and separated the camel and a shepherd who had by now come to blows. She said loudly in that very authoritarian way specific to infant teachers and traffic wardens, "And all the animals slept peacefully."

We stopped and looked at her. She repeated her sentence this time giving us all 'The Look' and we subsided into the straw. The play finished with one angel and a mute Mary who had to be dubbed by Brown Owl but otherwise without a hitch. When it came to the bows we four moved to the front of the stage to ecstatic cheers and clapping. It was truly our finest hour.

By now we had reached High Spy and allowed ourselves a snack stop of precisely four minutes - I had a schedule to keep. Jacko and I shared a huge piece of Spar Madeira cake and Kath tucked into her smoked salmon and humus on a bagel. Thus recharged we made the gentle decent down to Maiden Moor occasionally breaking out into snatches of Gilbert and Sullivan as the theatrical theme continued. Three Little Maids never sounded as good as it did on a crisp February morning on the fellside. Catbells was next and rewarded our efforts with fabulous views over Derwent Water. Keswick was in sight and we were on time.

We meandered down the northern tip of Catbells and into the little forest walk marked on the map as Allerdale Ramble. "You know," I said to Kath, "the fell runners don't come this way, they drop off Robinson onto the road and run along along the tarmac for miles on end."

73

"Why?" asked Kath.

"Well Robinson is their last fell so I suppose it makes sense."

"Since when did fell running ever make sense?" she replied.

"Well it got us here."

As we opened the little kissing gate onto the path near the footbridge we became excited. We had fifteen minutes to get up the main street and touch the clock tower. Obviously unlike any Bob Graham I had attended their wouldn't be crowds of people cheering us in and wrapping us up in blankets but hey that didn't matter, we had done it.

We looked back over the two-year epic.

"Best day?" I asked.

"Definitely the Dodds ridge," she replied "You?"

"Probably the same but I also really enjoyed our dash up and down Fairfield."

"Best peak?" I asked.

"Steeple" she replied and I had to agree.

"Best person we met?" I countered.

Obviously the man who gave us bed and board but the Birkett's chap comes a very close second. Again we both agreed.

"Worst moment?" I queried.

"Bloody Lord's Rake. You?" she answered without hesitation.

"Bloody Skiddaw" I replied with equal vehemence, "Although realising that I had locked the keys in the wrong car was pretty bad and telling you about it was worse."

We had reached the clock tower with three minutes to spare. I reached out to touch it.

"Worth it?" I asked lifting a bemused Jacko up so that he could touch the tower with his tired little paw.

"Definitely" she smiled and again we were in full agreement.

Epilogue

Name of Top	Date Climbed	Date of your climb and comments
1. Skiddaw	15.08.94	
2. Great Calva	15.08.94	
3. Blencathra	15.08.94	
4. Clough Head	17.09.94	
5. Great Dod	17.09.94	
6. Watson Dod	17.09.94	
7. Stybarrow Dod	17.09.94	
8. Raise	17.09.94	
9. Whiteside	17.09.94	
10. Hellvelyn Lower Man	17.09.94	
11. Hellvelyn	17.09.94	
12. Nethermost Pike	17.09.94	
13. Dollywaggon Pike	17.09.94	
14. Fairfield	19.04.95	
15. Seat Sandal	17.09.94	
16. Steel Fell	02.11.94	
17. Calf Crag	02.11.94	
18. High Raise	02.11.94	
19. Sergeant Man	02.11.94	
20. Thunacar Knotts	02.11.94	
21. Harrison Stickle	02.11.94	
22. Pike O stickle	02.11.94	
23. Rossett Pike	20.04.95	
24. Bowfell	02.07.95	
25. Esk pike	02.07.95	
26. Great End	02.07.95	
27. Ill Crag	02.07.95	
28. Broad End	02.07.95	
29. Scafell Pike	02.07.95	
30. Scafell	02.07.95	
31. Yewbarrow	30.08.95	
32. Red Pike	30.08.95	
33. Steeple	30.08.95	
34. Pillar	30.08.95	
35. Kirk Fell	29.05.96	
36. Great Gable	30.10.95	

37. Green Gable	30.10.95
38. Brandreth	30.10.95
39. Grey Knotts	30.10.95
40. Dale Head	28.08.96
41. Hindscarth	28.08.96
42. Robinson	28.08.96
Keswick for the 2nd time	08.02.97

The Last Word

So what happened next? Kath and Steve are still together and considering their ignominious start they have one of the strongest relationships I know. They are still very dear friends and regular walkers. I got promoted to a job that robbed me of all my spare time and very nearly both my sanity and my soul. I moved on, brought a huge chestnut ex-racehorse (Jacko spent much of his old age sat on a pile of horse blankets in the trailer glaring at other dogs and escaping to beg at the burger van). I still walk when I have time and find it a comfort to know that the fells are there waiting for me. Derek continues to back horses that almost win and continues to run up hills that should be ambled up.

Jacko died in May 2002 at 17 years old, still overweight, still cantankerous... still missed. RIP. I'm sure there will be left over sandwiches and wide open fells in doggy heaven.

But this book is not just about people and animals; it's about the fells and their capacity to soothe, to inspire awe, to calm and to terrify. They are timeless and glorious and they fill me with a range of hopes. I hope that they are never mined or quarried again for some mineral that fashion suddenly dictates as essential. I hope they retain the real element of danger and are not tamed into theme parks with funicular railways, chair lifts and way-marked tarmac paths. I hope they do not become cluttered with burger bars and shops selling mint cake, stuffed, woolly, smiling herdwicks and tee shirts saying 'I've climbed Skiddaw'. I hope no one from the MLC assessment group reads this book and decide to rescind my pass. I hope one day that Nature Appreciation replaces Technology on the National Curriculum. I hope Sellafield is as safe as it claims to be. I hope you read this book and are inspired to enjoy the splendour of these tops and then again I hope you're not. I hope they remain free for all, not the expensive playground of the fee paying few who have to pay tolls to go onto their slopes. I hope they survive this so-called civilisation and are still there to be enjoyed by the next one, which I hope will have learned from our mistakes.

For more Hayloft books, see:

www.hayloft.eu

or write to:
Hayloft Publishing Ltd., South Stainmore, Kirkby Stephen,
Cumbria, CA17 4DJ, UK.
Please enclose a cheque plus £2 for UK postage and packing.

or telephone: +44 (0)17683) 42300